HELP!
I'M GRIEVING!
DEALING WITH THE PROCESS

DENNIS L. MARTIN

HELP! I'M GRIEVING!
DEALING WITH THE PROCESS

To contact the author:
Dennis L. Martin, Sr.
4550 Jonesboro Rd Ste A2 104
Union City, Georgia 30291
Office: (770) 629-7883
Mobile Office: (470) 223-5040
Website: www.dlmartin.org

ISBN: 978-1-66788-231-4

Printed in the United States of America

Table of Contents

ACKNOWLEDGEMENTS

First, I want to thank my wife, Lady June Pace Martin, for her continued love, support, and sacrifice during our 43 years of marriage. I love you so much!

I would like to thank my daughter, Anthalena P. Martin, and my son, Dennis (DL) Martin, Jr., for the love, support, and encouragement they have given me over the years. I also thank you both for giving your time to help me do ministry. To my daughter- in-love, Mae Martin, thanks for coming into my life and showing love as if I were your biological father. Also, I am deeply grateful for my grandchildren, Madison, D3, Rylee, and King. You all are such a blessing to me.

I give special thanks to Bishop Liza Hickman for taking on this project, putting things in order and sharing her words of wisdom. I would not have moved forward without her encouraging me to get this done. I am also grateful to Sister Angela McLeod for her professional eyes in reviewing this book and helping me express the sentiments of my heart.

I am grateful for the members of Restoration Revival Ministries Church of God in Christ. I thank God for allowing me to be your pastor for 27 years. Thank you all!

Finally, I dedicate this book to the memory of my loved ones who have gone on before me. They include my mother, Barbara Ann Armstrong; my grandmother, Olena Martin; my uncle, Rev. Gene Martin, my father-in-law, Superintendent Murphy Pace, Jr., my brother-in-law, Bishop M.J. Pace, III, my mother-in-law, Mother Bettie Ann Pace, my sisters, Duranice Pace and LaShun Pace, Bishop G.E. Patterson and Mother Louise Patterson and so many other family and friends that have gone on before me. May God always bless their memory!

Introduction

Hello, and how are you doing? Let's have a talk. I know you've been dealing with the loss and grief of someone near and dear to you. That's why you picked up this book.

Hey, I have been there too, and I have talked with hundreds of people going through situations, perhaps similar to yours, and they need some answers. They desire understanding and some support in dealing with and getting through grief. On, my Check - In Monday Live program, we have dealt with this very real subject, and this book summarizes those talks. Many of the viewers asked me to compile those conversations so they could have them for encouragement along the way to recovery.

Listen, I am not a clinician. I am a Pastor and a real person who has had some serious and heart-wrenching losses. Within the pages of this book, I have been transparent in telling my personal stories and the stories of others who have dealt with grief. Also, I am sharing how to manage and cope while you're going through it. We all have some things in common when it comes to the subject of grief and losses. I hope that you can connect and identify. On the other hand, we are all different and will handle our grief differently.

It is, however, my prayer that the wisdom and stories shared with you here will offer you understanding and comfort and help you to deal with grief in a very real way. Be assured that I will keep it real, aiming to help by having this conversation. If it does help and make a difference, I request that you join me in helping many others by sharing this invaluable information that has made a positive change for you.

So, imagine me sitting down across from you, at the kitchen table, face to face and sharing heart to heart. Now let's get this conversation started....

CHAPTER 1

LORD, I DON'T UNDERSTAND

Many times, in church, we've been taught to put our trust in God. Most of us do trust and believe Him, but there comes a time in life when things happen that make you say to yourself, "I trust God, but I don't get it. I just don't understand". You pray and ask God about it. You want answers and you want to know what is going on. Sometimes God gives you an answer, and sometimes He doesn't. There may have been times that He gave you the answers ahead of the circumstance at hand, but you did not recognize them, see them, or pay attention to them. You are left saying again, "I just don't get it. I don't understand. God, what in the world is going on?" There are times when you have a sense of what to expect, based on the conditions and circumstances you are dealing with. In those cases, I think all of us can better prepare for death because we sense it is coming and have some time to prepare for that outcome. For example, a loved one who is sick, you anticipate that if God doesn't heal them, they're not going to survive. In that situation, if things turn for the worse, you can start to deal with the prospect of their death. Even though the loss will still be a devastating loss, you can deal with it a little better because you had time to adjust and prepare. However, when tragedy happens suddenly, it has a greater impact of shock, loss, and pain.

Untimely or unexpected death happens when you are not anticipating it to happen, such as a car accident, murder, fatal heart attack, or aneurysm. It can be very hard to deal with this type of situation. We could have been talking to the person on Monday, then, the next day, we got the news that they are no longer with us. We were not looking for it to happen.

My cousin's husband died in 2014. I knew my uncle Gene was in town, and I just knew he was going to be at the homegoing service. When he didn't attend the service, I knew something was wrong, but I just brushed it off. One week later, my cousin called and told me that my uncle was sick and hospitalized. We went to the hospital every day to check on him. Eventually, they put him in a home for extended care. After he was transferred to the home, I developed the routine of visiting him every day.

My uncle lost his sight and therefore could only hear us talk. One day he told us "Everybody should come to see me before next week, because I will not be here next week. The Lord showed it to me". He gave us a timeframe of when he was going to pass. We listened to him, but I don't think we grasped how accurate he was in making that statement. The timeframe he gave us happened just like he said. We had time to prepare for that mentally and emotionally, yet it still affected us. It still does today. March 20 of every year, the day that he passed, still affects me. His birthday is April 24, and we would always talk to each other on our birthdays. My uncle used to call me and wish me a happy birthday no matter where he was in the world. I don't get those calls anymore. I'm still affected by his death, but my point is that although he passed away, I had time to sort of prepare for my grieving process, simply because I knew that he was going to eventually leave us, because of what he told us. The grieving process was still challenging.

Another thing that helped me with my uncle's passing was that he was always on the go, moving from one town to another. He wasn't married. For all our lives, he traveled, and I used to travel with him. We may have seen him three to four times a year because he was on the road all the time, preaching and singing. We talked on the phone, but not seeing him every day was one thing that helped me through the process. Even after he died, it almost felt like he was still just out of town.

Another friend of mine, Pastor Stephan Henderson, from Chicago, would call me every now and then and we would talk about the Church. He would call and say, "Hey, Pastor, how are you doing?" I miss our conversations. I miss our dialogues about the church happenings, family and ministry. He's not here!! I've also noticed that one of his close friends from his youth would post something almost every day. He posted a picture of them from way back and he added the text, "Man, I miss this guy." You know what, that is okay.

11

Now the process may be different with each death that you may face. In my mother's case, she had been sick and in and out of the hospital for a while. As a result, processing that situation and grieving occurred differently. Whenever someone has a lengthy illness, it may be easier to brace yourself for their transition.

When my brother-in-law, Bishop Pace, passed, he was in the hospital but had been released to go home, and I would go by the house and talk with him. About a week before he passed, we spoke, and the day before he died, I dropped my wife, Lady Martin, off at her mother's house and Bishop was staying there. The next morning, about six or seven o'clock in the morning, the phone rang. I don't know how you feel, but I get a sense that something may have happened when my phone rings early in the morning. We answered the phone, and my wife's sister was on the other end, saying "The Lord said He had received Bishop with honors". We asked, "What does that mean?", and she said, "Well, he passed away". This was a sudden death. We were not expecting him to die. We didn't have time to prepare at all.

My sister, Shawn Pair, husband passed away three years ago, and it was an untimely passing, and she is still grieving over the loss of her husband. So many times, people say you need to get over it and get a life. Well, it's easy to say that if you've never been through that particular process and lost someone significant or someone close to you. Sometimes, you don't know how to deal with those things until you have been in that place. Grieving and going through that process can take a while. Even though you function every day and don't stop, you are still going through that process of grieving and dealing with an unexpected death. When someone has had a lengthy illness, sometimes you can absorb that a little quicker and move on a little faster, but when it's a sudden death or tragic loss, it takes a little more time. When your spouse passes unexpectedly, or a mother must bury her daughter or grandchild who passed unexpectedly, it takes longer to get through that process. No mother or father expects to bury their child. It is often difficult when you have to say goodbye to a young person who has so much life ahead of them. The truth is, we just don't expect death to come so suddenly. Anything could happen today or tomorrow, and when you're dealing with a sudden death you are left feeling numb. It leaves you feeling distraught. You get distracted, and things bother you a little more. Sometimes people don't understand, especially if they have not experienced similar losses. You can't hold it against them. They don't understand what it's like going through the funeral planning and the homegoing service, as we call it, along with the other things we do to celebrate the life of our deceased ones. Meanwhile, you are still in shock through all of this. In these times since the pandemic has started, we haven't always been able to have complete services for closure. The pandemic has at times prevented ceremonies, funerals or memorial services, therefore, preventing those from getting the closure they needed.

There is a different sense of grieving from the unexpected, untimely death of someone healthy. I remember my church mother (now deceased), her son was healthy, vibrant, strong, and only 50 years old. He got sick suddenly, went into the hospital, and never came out. His mother and his sisters were devastated. They were trying to understand, "Where did that come from? That just doesn't seem to make sense!"

Untimely deaths make you wonder, and ask God, "What in the world is going on"? I don't get it. I just don't, and I can't comprehend it." Even though we've been taught not to question God and not to ask God anything about why He allows this, we are compelled to ask God. Let me share this with you: If you don't ask God, and if you don't question Him, how will you know? How can He give you the answers if you don't ask Him? Go ahead and ask God, "What is this? What happened? Why?" We trust God to provide the answers. We're not asking Him with an attitude or a bad disposition. Sometimes you just want to know, "God what are you doing? What are you saying?" For example, this is what recently happened in the case of my sister, Duranice. She was on the set for the movie about Aretha Franklin's life. She cut her hand, so she went to the hospital, and they admitted her. After being there for a few days, she came home, and then she had to go back for something that wasn't related to her initial reason for going to the hospital. She was not so ill to the extent that we were anticipating her passing away. When we got the call that she had transitioned, it made no sense.

It made me wonder for several reasons, "Lord what is going on?" It did not make sense to me. Her dream of being on Broadway was finally happening. She was on her way to Broadway!! There were producers interested in taking her "One-Woman Show" to the next level. They were in collaboration with Duranice. They even started the process on that project and several others. I was shaken and shocked by her sudden passing. I said to God, "I don't understand". You may be in such a place too saying to God, "I just don't understand." I want to honestly tell you, it's okay not to understand everything! It's okay not to understand what and why! I'm going to say it one more time, "It's okay not to understand everything!"

Sometimes, we put ourselves under a lot of pressure because we feel we need to understand what God has done, even though we trust Him. In the year 2000, I'll never forget when I got a phone call early one morning, informing me that my niece, LaShun's daughter, Xenia, had taken ill at school and an ambulance was called to take her to the hospital. I rushed to the school, and they said she was already taken to the hospital. That morning, walking into the hospital, they took me back to the room where her mother was sitting. When I walked in, there was my niece, 11 years old, lying on that table, stiff, cold, and passed away. I'll never forget her mother looking up at me saying, "Pastor, talk to me. Talk to me, please talk to me." I will never forget that conversation. At that moment, the words of the late Mom Marlene Tally came back to me. I'll never forget saying to LaShun, "We have to trust God. We don't understand and we don't know why God would allow this, but Mom Tally said we trust her into the hands of a God that never makes a mistake."

Wow! Think about that, **WE TRUST HER INTO THE HANDS OF A GOD THAT NEVER MAKES A MISTAKE!**

He may give us understanding somewhere down the road, or He may not give us understanding at all. If He does, we'll thank Him, but if He doesn't, we can trust our loved ones into the hands of a God that never makes a mistake. I thought about it like this: "God, I trust you enough to believe that you don't make mistakes. I trust you enough to believe, whether it's with Duranice or with one of my other loved ones". We don't know why God does what He does. That's why I stopped trying to figure God out. I just trust Him and just believe Him. He has already told us that His ways are not our ways, and His thoughts are not our thoughts. The way we think is not the way God is thinking. We just have to trust God, regardless. We've got to believe Him and just say, "God, I trust you. I don't know how this will turn out. I don't know why, but I trust you, and since you don't think the way I think, I just got to believe that you know what you're doing!"

Why is it that God will allow one to go into the hospital

16

with COVID-19, and He brings them out, but another one goes in, and they never come out? I don't know. All I know is we have to trust in God. I tell you, when I contracted COVID-19 and was hospitalized, I prayed that God would bring me out of the hospital, and He did. Others also prayed, but they didn't make it out, and we don't understand. When you don't understand, don't put a lot of pressure on yourself. Don't stress yourself out trying to figure out what God is doing, or why He's doing it. Sometimes, we don't even know when people are in certain situations if they have asked God to take them out of here. I've seen people that prayed and said, Lord, I'm ready to go home. I've seen people hold their loved ones here even when they were prepared to go. They wouldn't release them because it was hard to let them go.

Once, a young lady at my church was requesting prayer on a Tuesday night. She was concerned about her grandmother. The young lady had moved to Atlanta from Memphis. She was going to move her grandmother from Memphis to Atlanta to take care of her grandmother. She was getting ready to move her the next day. However, that Tuesday night, the Lord had me to say to her, "I know you want your grandmother here, but the Lord told me to tell you that you need to let your grandmother go. Your grandmother is ready to go and be with the Lord, and you are the holdup. You're the one holding her up from going." She burst into tears and cried. She said, "Okay, I'm going to let her go." She released her grandmother to go on Tuesday night. The next day, her grandmother transitioned.

Sometimes we don't know if the person we are holding on to is waiting on us to release them. When my grandmother Olena was living, my uncle Gene Martin cared for her and took good care of her. My uncle was drafting a book at the time. In the book he was writing, he was talking about grandmother Olena. He was pressing himself to get done with the book. The Lord spoke to him, instructing him to name the book in memory of my grandmother. Of course, he didn't like to hear that. He immediately said, "I rebuke that. That's the devil, and I rebuke that", and the Lord let him know that he needed to let her go. He was the holdup. He told him, "She's ready to go. She's tired. She's ready to leave, but you are praying that she stays here." Because he wouldn't release her, he got ill and could not finish the book. My grandmother said to my Uncle Gene, "My boy, Gene, you are holding me up." When he finally let her go, she made the transition.

It's not always for us to understand, and I know that's a difficult thing. Even though sometimes God gives us signs and he says little things to us, we don't want to hear those things, and we sort of push Him away and say, "That's not you. That's the devil"! Sometimes, God is letting us know he's getting ready to do something. Something is getting ready to take place. We have to change the way we think. I'm going to say this, and it may disturb some of you or make some of you upset, but I think in some instances, churches have done a bad job on certain things. One of the things is our understanding of death and the loss of a loved one.

It's okay for us not to have all the answers. It's okay for us not to pretend we've got all the answers. Really, it's okay. I know you don't believe that, but we don't have the answers to everything. Even if we pray and fast, we don't have the answers to everything. If someone asks you something that you don't have the answer to, it's okay to say you don't have the answer to that. That was Job's dilemma. Job did not have the answer to what he was going through. The Bible tells us what kind of man he was, and he didn't understand. That's why he went through what he went through. God finally came and talked to him, and that was a great thing, but Job said, "I don't get it". If Job would have known that all he went through was because the devil questioned God about him, maybe he would have dealt with it differently, but he didn't understand, and he didn't know. It's hard sometimes, and that's the human side of it. We need to realize that we are spiritual, but we're human too. Someone once said to me that when a loved one passes, I shouldn't be crying. They told me that I should be the man of God and be this and be that. I ignored them because I understood that they didn't understand. On the human side, even Jesus wept. If Jesus cried, we certainly can cry.

When you understand that if you don't understand, it's okay, you will be better. I remind you that it's okay if we don't have all the answers. I don't have them. I'm not going to tell you I've got them. I'm not going to pretend I know why. I'm not going to fake it or try to act so spiritual. You see, I'm still dealing with loved ones and people that have passed that were close to me. I'm still dealing with that and every day I'm trying to figure out, Lord, what was that? I just don't get that.

I start looking at people who passed who were not sick or ill. I saw one of the pastors online, from here in Atlanta, who passed. I didn't know him, but he was planning some things. He was talking about 21 days, and they were going to be doing something big. Despite his plans, he passed suddenly of a heart attack. As I mentioned before, one of my good friends, Pastor Stephan Henderson, was only 49 years old when he passed. I watched his Bible study online the night before, and he looked fine, and he talked about Sunday service plans. Next thing I knew, I'm getting the call that he passed the next day. While in the hospital, the thing that was going through my mind was how quickly that could happen. Again, we don't have all the answers. If you don't understand, don't let anybody force you, push you, or cause you to go through changes. Don't let church people try to make you feel they have all the answers. They don't. Don't let the Pastor, prophet, prophetess, or anybody make you feel bad, because the truth is, we don't have all the answers.

Let's continue to pray for one another. Let's continue to call each other's names out. Let's continue checking in with one another and checking on one another. If someone comes in your heart very hard, don't put it off, reach out to them. We are still going to have to trust God in the end. Really trust Him!! Again, I want you to remember that the late Mom Tally put that thing in my spirit. **WE TRUST THEM IN THE HANDS OF A GOD THAT NEVER MAKES A MISTAKE.** God never makes a mistake. He knows what He's doing. We would love to have our loved ones here with us for a long time, but that's not always the case.

I want to help someone understand that you are not abnormal. You are very normal. People may make you feel like you're not normal. You're just as normal as normal can be. Every one of us have to walk down this path at some point in our life. I know you probably don't believe this, but I'm going to tell you anyway. You are going to be alright. You may be saying, "Now pastor, you just don't know, I just don't know." I promise you that you're going to be okay. Whether it's a loss of your mother, your father, husband, wife, children, you're going to be okay. I have not experienced some of those losses, but I do know that at the end of the day, God's going to make sure that you and I come through. I believe I'm going to be okay and you're going to be okay too.

"I cannot trust in a political system. The world is so rough that it's cold, finding just where they are barely existing. You're the only thing right left in a wrong world." [Marvin, Ron and Carvin Winans] God, we trust you!

CHAPTER 2

I NEVER THOUGHT I'D BE SAYING THIS RIGHT NOW

Who knew that in 2020, we would experience a pandemic that would divide us? Who could have imagined that we would not be able to meet in person for various holidays and do all those things that we traditionally do with one another? Many utilized virtual technology like Zoom and Facetime to see their family members. Now, so many are seeing one another face to face and we're getting back to gathering again, but still not fully as we once did.

Before the pandemic, I lost many dear people close to me, and once the pandemic hit, I lost a lot of people. One night, I did a homegoing celebration service for my cousin's wife. Now, here we are talking about grieving. I want to tell you that we've been in a strange and difficult place. You couldn't have told me that I would have gone through 2020 and lost so many friends and so many people that were close to me. You couldn't have made me believe that. You couldn't have told me that coming into 2021 and 2022, that we would still be losing so many people, family and friends. Honestly, there are times when I wonder if I am dreaming and need to wake up. An old

TV show comes to mind. Perhaps you're old enough to remember the Twilight Zone. The Twilight Zone depicted things that happened that were so strange that you could hardly believe them or couldn't put your mind around them. Have you ever stood in a place that looked like you were standing in the Twilight Zone? Are you finding yourself in that place that is real, but it's hard to believe it's happening? You may be thinking that you never would have imagined that you'd be in this place right now.

There are family members who can say that they never thought that they would be dealing with such tragedy in their families and in their lives. So many people have not lost just one family member, they've lost many family members. I've talked to people who've lost seven or eight family members, whether it was from the virus or whether it was a senseless murder.

When I went to my cousin's Homegoing celebration, her cousin stood up to have comments along with friends. The main theme of the night was that many people could not believe they were standing there, discussing death, and that they weren't prepared for it. At the service, the question was asked, "Well, how's everyone doing?" My response was that they seemed to be doing okay, the best that they could be, considering the circumstances.

Even though people mean well, sometimes people can't really help you to deal with loss when they don't know how to help. For example, when a wife has lost her husband, I can try to console her, quote the Scripture, and tell her what the Bible says and what I think will help her, but I really can't feel her level of loss. I can't feel her loss because I'm a man. Even if there is another lady who is offering to console and help, that lady has not experienced losing a husband and is sleeping next to her husband every night. That person really can't relate in that area, and the help she can offer may also be limited. Such is the case in losing a spouse, parent, child, or sibling. I can talk to you, but I really can't feel what you're feeling. I don't understand that depth of loss. I can talk to you, but I may not feel that pain. I may not understand how you feel, although I want to be helpful. I've never been in that place before. Sometimes we don't know what to say because we've never experienced that specific situation, so our ability to help is limited.

Sometimes death is not anticipated, but to deal with it, your mind races and you ask yourself whether it's something you could have prevented. You wonder if there is something you could have done. Is there some way you could have helped them. You will eventually realize that there is nothing that you could have done or said. You just never thought that this would be the case.

A church member was grieving because her niece was being bullied. The niece couldn't take it and killed herself. That was a rough place to be in. I had to talk to the member because it was tough. If you have never been there, you don't know how that feels, but it's got to be rough.

I have a member who is a twin. They've been around each other all their lives and her sister passed two years ago. She never thought that she would be dealing with not having her sister with her.

It looks like Facebook has now become the electronic obituary. It can get depressing to even look at the timelines. These are not only older people, but also the young, and some of them look like they had promising futures. You may find yourself in disbelief about having to post a message or have a certain conversation. When they called me Saturday night and told me about Apostle Nicks, I asked, "Who?" I had to wonder if I was hearing the right things because you think your ears are playing tricks on you. You would hope that nobody would take a joke to that extent. You keep saying to yourself, I know this can't be real. Then, you find out that it is real, and it actually happened.

I must say this until somebody gets it in their spirit. We've got to love each other while we've got each other. Tomorrow is not promised to any of us. I think that it's time for us to take a different look at how we look at one another. Take a different look at how we approach one another. I know some people hurt you. I know some people did you wrong, and you thought they would never do that. I get it, but I want to tell you, the way things are going, we can't afford to keep holding on to grudges and unforgiveness.

I know we think we're going to be here a long time. We don't know that for sure. The other week when Pastor Green from Virginia died, that thing hit me so hard. I had just talked to him about a week and a half before he passed. We were working on a project together. He called and wanted me to do a presentation, but I was unable to do it at that time. Then, someone called and asked me if my phone had been ringing. I told them I had not received phone calls, and when they gave me the news, it knocked the wind out of me for a minute. I asked, "What did you say? Are you serious?"

I've known people to wake up, have a heart attack and by noon, the same day, they had died. It's unbelievable. So, what you and I must do is drop some of the pettiness that keeps us divided, at odds, and unforgiving. Some of this stuff is so petty. A phone call would take care of it, a lunch or dinner meeting, or just an apology. We need to just admit that we are wrong and ask for forgiveness. Aim to resolve those unsettled things. It doesn't mean that you have to hang out with the person every day. We do know that at any moment, any of us can be out of here, and we want to get things right while we have the chance.

I got a different resolve in August 2020. When I had COVID-19 and was admitted to the hospital, I couldn't believe that I was there because I never had to be in the hospital overnight. I was in a state of shock that I was actually there. I was going through changes. Every time I got a call or every time my wife and my children would FaceTime me, I was watching my grandson King, hoping he would start walking soon, and I didn't want to miss that. He did start walking when

I got home from the hospital, and I was happy about that. While there in the hospital, I was thinking about some stuff that I was trying to finish in the house, and I was asking the Lord to please let me get back home. I kept saying, "I need to get back home to my family and ministry," but while I was in the hospital, I had a transformation. My wife says to me every day "Something happened to you in that hospital." When I ask what she means, she says she can't explain it, but she is sure that I have changed. She has said that I'm a different person since I came out of the hospital. She says that nothing was wrong with me before, but there's something that has changed me. I told her that while I was there, I got a reality check. What was your reality check, Pastor Martin?

Here's my reality check. Sometimes we feel we're invincible. We think that nothing can touch us. Nothing can bother us. The reality is, I'm lying in the hospital, with these tubes in my nose and all these IVs and nurses sticking me and giving me medicine, knowing that my only hope is not the medicine, but God's miracle working power. I'm glad they gave me what they did and could give to help me, but my only hope was for God to bring me out of there. I knew if He brought me out, I could see my family and friends again. I could do the right things. He gave me a second chance to do what needed to be done before I went into the hospital. So, today I have no disputes with anybody. I don't go through any changes. I'm not fighting with anybody. I'm trying to make sure I understand and keep my mind focused every day. The reality is that any day could be your last day. You could lay down and not get up. You could go out and have an accident and be killed. So, again, I'm not going to have a dispute with you. I love you, and there is nothing you can do about it. You don't even have to love me back. I still love you anyway. So, I appeal to all that we should love one another.

Whether it's with family, friends, co-workers, or anyone else, we should get things that have caused separation together and in order. Go and deal with that thing. Deal with it! Get things together! Do what you need to do and be at peace. Give yourself peace. I can't control what anyone else thinks. I can't control what anyone else does. I can only control myself and what I do. So, it's my responsibility to treat people right. I'm not being deep. Too much is going on, and we must deal with it. So, let's love each other. Let's keep praying for one another. Call to check on your family and friends. I want to encourage you to do the right thing. I don't know how much longer this pandemic is going to last or when the next wave of something else is coming our way, but these times tell us that life is filled with swift transitions. We never know where our timeline finishes. Life is like a vapor. David declared that there's but a step between me and death. I love all my family and friends. I love those that even think that we are enemies. Life is too short not to care for one another.

Again, I just want to encourage you while you are facing the crisis of death and loss. I promise you that we are going to come out of this. As I was driving the car, my daughter was talking with someone on the phone, a young lady battling cancer. She had her phone on speaker, and the young lady was talking about all the things she was going through. She said something that caught my attention that I couldn't get out of my spirit. The young lady battling cancer said these words and I am leaving them with you. She said, **"I'm coming out on the other side of this."** That thing dropped in my spirit, and I haven't been able to get it out. That's been at least a year and a half ago. Be encouraged and know that despite what's going on and whatever you're going through, we're coming out on the other side of this.

CHAPTER 3

WHEN THE REALITY OF IT ALL SETS IN

When loss first happens, most of us are busy trying our best to put things in place and get things in order. We make sure programs are together and we reach out to relatives and friends and to those who were close. People come by your house and share with you and talk with you. You have some moments where you laugh and cry together. Before the pandemic, you would have a repass or dinner. You hear people say that they are going to be there for you. After all those events are over, now you have some downtime. You're not busy doing things, and so now the reality that this person is gone hits you. They're not coming back, and you're not going to talk to them again, they're not coming out of the room, and they're not going to visit your home. This can be one of the most challenging parts of grieving, when you've seen them for the last time. At home, absence is real, especially if the person lived with you. There is no doubt you were close and talked every day. You now must get in mind that they're no longer here. There's nothing wrong with the fact that you are struggling to deal with them not being here to talk to or answer the phone when you call. Dealing with the reality of their absence is another level of grief and it will be hard at times. Now, you have to face the fact that you've never been without them before. You may ask how can you deal with this, how can you move on, and how do you process this. It is an emotional process that you have to deal with, and people will make you feel that it's not. Still, it's very emotional when you are dealing with the loss of a mother, father, sister, brother, a friend, someone that was close, someone that you were able to share your secrets with or share the things that were dear to your heart. You're not able to share with them now because that person is gone. That comfort is no longer there, and you don't have that person to lean on. Many times, that's the part that makes it a hard reality, along with everything else that follows. We've got to deal with the things that are left, such as their clothing, taking care of their accounts for them, and being head of the estate, etc. We've got to go through all of their things that have been accumulated. We've got to decide if we're going to give their things away or hold onto them for a time or not get rid of them at all. It's a reality. I hear some of you are in the same place I was. I was mad at God for a long time, having been left to deal with what was left. There are people that are angry with God right now. Remember the young lady I mentioned before that's a member of my church, whose sister died, and they were twins, she just told me that she didn't know how to deal with God. I didn't rebuke her. I understood. She's coming around. But some people just don't understand.

So, these are the realities of that hardest part of grieving. Now, you've got to deal with these things as they come and as they are. I know we don't like to talk about this, but some people are dealing with this in a way that if they're not careful, can shift over to depression. As I was preparing to talk about this, I had a conversation with my wife. I said, "Tell me, what is the hardest part of this for you? Because you know, people tell you when the services and stuff are over, I'm a phone call away. All you have to do is call me and whatever." She said something that I had never thought about, and something I think will help a lot of us, that was so profound. She said these words, "I know they want to help us and I know they want to be there for us. I believe that, but I also know that it may not be convenient for them to be there when it hits me because this thing has no time. You have no control over when it hits you. You have no control when you have to deal with it." I started thinking about that because that's true. Sometimes you can't control when grief hits you. You can't control when you feel a certain kind of way. It might hit you at 3:30 in the morning. You can't call people. My wife said it might hit you at 2:00 am in the morning. That's true. You may be in your bed feeling fine, and then, suddenly, that thing hits you, and it's at a time that you can't even call your family or friends. You may be just lying in the bed with tears flowing down your eyes. You may be weeping, crying, and thinking, and sometimes you've got to get up and find something to do to occupy your time. It can hit you, not only just at home, but it can also hit you at your job or in the strangest places. It can hit you so hard until you have to find a place to go where people won't look at you crazy and funny. I've experienced that it could be months later, and it may just hit you in the middle of the day, and you break down. You can't explain to people why you're crying. You can't explain to people why you feel a certain way.

Let me tell you something vital. I think, if you get this, you'll be a whole lot better. Stop always looking for people to understand where you are in your grieving process. Everyone will not get it. Everyone will not understand it. If they've never experienced it, they will never be able to tell you how to deal with something they've never experienced. If they experienced grief, they may be able to relate in some ways to what's going on, but even then, no two people are alike. When people don't understand they really just don't understand. They will make you feel bad because they don't know how to say what needs to be said. They don't know what it is they need to say to you. So, when they don't know what they need to say, sometimes they will say something that may be too far over, inconsiderate, and insensitive. Sometimes people will tell you to just think of the good parts. We do those things, but missing a person is still difficult to deal with. Sometimes we don't have people to talk to, and you don't have people that sometimes understand. For some reason, everyone wants us to get over everything so quickly. No, we're not going to wallow in grief forever. Don't get me wrong. We will move from that place. It'll get better as time goes on. I told you that time heals a lot of things, but you know sometimes rushing and trying to make believe something is not there will take you to a place where you could lose touch with reality.

I watched one of my favorite shows the other night, Perry Mason, and the plot was that a lady's baby had died. They made it look like the baby had been kidnapped. The baby hadn't been kidnapped. The baby had just died. When they came back from paying the ransom, the lady said, "The baby is back." She went up into the room, and they followed her. She said, "Look at him in his crib. My baby is back! My baby is back!" They looked at each other because the crib was empty, but the lady had gone to a place that wasn't reality. She saw a baby in the bed that wasn't there. Sometimes, you know, when people don't deal with the reality of things, then false reality takes over.

My uncle has been dead for six years. He died on March 20, 2015. I was out today in my garage, and I have some of his stuff there. I've got some of his things at church. I've got all his sermon books, about 20 or 30 of them. I have all his books, and I've gone through some of them, and I'll go through all of them eventually. At the church, in my office, I have about ten containers of CDs because he used to collect CDs and records. I've got all his clothing. I've got his shoes. I've got his robes. I've got his Bibles. I've got almost all the things he had. Eventually, I'll get to sit down and go through all of it because I know he just collected this stuff. He collected over 1000 records and albums. Even though about six years have passed,

I haven't gone through all his stuff yet. Will I go through it? Hopefully, I plan on it, but I just don't know when. Perhaps, like me, you may not get to everything at once because it's too hard. The reality sets in that I've got to deal with this, and you can choose the best time for you to do so, but eventually, you will need to do this.

Going through what has been left can be difficult because some things have an emotional attachment. People can get upset with you so easily over you holding on to items or things that your loved one has passed on to you. They want you to throw it away or give it to them. They might even demonize you and say terrible things because they do not understand that you cherish the items because of the loved one who gave them to you. My uncle gave me all those things before he passed. He gave me a whole collection of C. L. Franklin albums. I have an entire collection of Pastor Jasper Williams. I have an entire collection of the tape catalog of C. L. Franklin and the Davis Sisters albums. I am probably sitting on a goldmine here. My point is that he gave it to me, so it's precious to me. Now to somebody else, it means nothing. To somebody else, it's just some CDs. To somebody else, it's just some records. To somebody else, it could be just a ring. It could be just a table. It could be whatever. They just don't have the connection that you have, so it won't mean very much to them or it won't mean nothing at all.

It's hard for you to part with those things because they mean so much to you. You're saying that you just can't part with the things that were given to you. Some of these things are precious so you just can't throw them away. I understand it is difficult. We must talk about these things and deal with them. It's vital for us to know that if we are talking about it, if we are dealing with it, and if we share, this helps deal with the reality of all this. I want to encourage those of you who are entering into this phase. I want you to know you're going to make it, that you're going to be all right, and you're going to come through it.

Every one of us needs someone that understands. Sometimes you just need someone that can listen and understand or to talk to you. Just hear me out, you need someone who will let you get this off your chest when needed. You need someone to be there that would let you talk about the memories, and cherished things. On another note, whenever you're grieving, make sure that you pray. I know you don't feel like it all the time but do it anyway. Do not make important decisions without praying. Sometimes in the first part of the hard grieving, we can make decisions that will have a lasting effect on us. Sometimes you need to step back and not make any decisions right then. Sometimes you need to step back and say, I'm not going to make those decisions right now. I'm just going to sit back and be still and give myself a moment for clarity.

When you're grieving, sometimes, unfortunately, people take advantage of you. Also, people will bring you all kinds of things and offers. Because you're grieving, they can manipulate you while you are in a vulnerable state. I say to you, while you're grieving, please do not make major decisions that you don't have to make at that time. You should take your time and make your decisions, especially when dealing with money, or a settlement. Don't let everyone know that you have something. Don't tell the world.

Be encouraged and know that we're praying for you and know that things will get better. Time will bring about some resolve for some of these things, and you'll find out that you will come out alright. You'll come out better on the other side of this. Keep holding your head up. Keep doing what you must do. Watch God do something great for you!

CHAPTER 4

GIVE YOURSELF TIME TO GRIEVE AND HEAL

There is something you should do about grief. Give yourself time to grieve and time to heal. Many people try to rush you through the grieving process of healing, but remember it is a process. You must give yourself time to process those things that are taking place. What do I mean? For example, if you've ever had major surgery, you will find that you just don't have surgery and then come out of the hospital the next day and resume the same energy and the same strength you had before major surgery.

You must give yourself time to heal the same way it takes time physically to recover. That's why you have to go back to the doctor after you've been seen once. You go back, and they give you an assessment of your progress. I remember when I had major surgery on my ankle because I broke it in 2005 in two places. I didn't have to stay overnight, but they wrapped my ankle, and they said you cannot do anything. I couldn't put any pressure on it, so they gave me crutches. For two weeks I couldn't do anything, I had to be serviced. After a while, I was feeling some kind of way. So I went back to the doctors, and they told me that everything was

just fine. I just needed to keep doing what I was doing. Eventually, I went back, they took the wrap off, and then they put a cast on my ankle. From that point, I had to wear it for four weeks. About six weeks, I was not working or doing anything; this was my right ankle, my driving ankle, my driving foot, so I still couldn't do anything, anything at all. What happened while I was there, not doing anything on that ankle for six weeks? This was giving me time to heal.

Eventually, when they took the cast off, I thought it was done, but even with them taking the cast off, they gave me a boot to wear. I had to learn how to walk with that walking boot and then go through therapy to stretch my foot and my ankle, so I could use my ankle normally again. Healing takes time. Even today, I still have a pin and a plate in my right ankle with six screws. Even when my wife had surgery, and returned home, she could not go anywhere. She couldn't even go to church. She had to heal. In every case of major surgery there's a reason doctors send you home to do certain things. They want you to heal. Your body must heal so that you will fully recuperate.

You must give yourself time to grieve and heal when you're dealing with death. Don't let people make you feel that you have to rush back into life as usual. You must give yourself time to deal with what has happened. Give yourself time to deal with the process of your healing. People will have you thinking that you can get up and go right back into the activities you were doing before. Perhaps, some people can, but for most of us, it takes time. It takes time to heal from certain things. If you don't give yourself time to heal, you won't heal. When I got sick with COVID-19, I must admit that when I was released, I thought in my mind that I would do the things I was doing before I went into the hospital. I felt okay. I thought I was good. I came out, but then I noticed when I got home, I was still short of breath. I noticed when I got home, some things changed in just those ten days of being in the hospital, laying in that bed. My legs lost strength as far as walking. It took me from the time I was discharged from the hospital, all the way to the new year, to get my lungs back. Even when I did my first live stream right after I came out of the hospital, you couldn't tell it, but I was hoping I could make it through just that conversation. Why? Because I was not giving myself time to heal. I wanted to get back into preaching and doing the things I was doing before I got sick, but I discovered that I was not ready because my body was still healing. In addition to that, I wasn't giving myself time mentally to deal with the fact that I just came out of the hospital and almost died. Again, I had to give myself time to heal.

You must give yourself time, and that doesn't mean that you've got to become inactive, but it means that you've got to give yourself time to grieve. If you've lost a loved one, don't rush yourself. Give yourself time to meditate, to build up, and to do the things you have to do. People will pressure you into a nervous breakdown or a state of depression if you allow them to rush

The truth is, you can get depressed over the loss of that loved one, over the loss of what has happened. I don't want to sound like I'm criticizing the church, but in church especially, we try to make people rush through their process. You cannot rush through certain processes. Some things you must deal with, and you have to deal with them head-on. You have to deal with the reality of what's happened. You must take time to grieve!

This process is not going to be as quick. You'll find yourself doing things to occupy your time. If you don't give yourself time to heal, you'll find that you may experience worse things later on down the road, because you didn't give yourself time to heal.

There's a reason for having to give things time to run their course. When I used to go to the doctor, sometimes they gave me antibiotics. The doctor would tell me that I needed to take the full bottle of medication for the entire 14 days. I had to take them every day. One day, I asked my doctor why it was important to take all the medication. He said that even if I felt better after a few days or a few doses, the antibiotic could not do the full job of correcting the problem until all the medicine had been finished. Make sure you finish your grieving process, and then, you can say that you're healed.

Most of the time, we're so busy rushing the process of being healed that we become bitter and indifferent. We become angry, and our tolerance level is low. If you don't give yourself time to grieve and to heal, you may turn to that place of bitterness. Some people will say you just need to pray. I say let's allow their commentary until they have to deal with it. Then they will understand things better when it happens to them.

Prayer alone is not the only thing needed. Tell me how prayer works by itself. I believe in the power of prayer, but prayer alone is not the answer to your grief. When you've lost a loved one, you've got to deal with an emotional roller coaster. You can pray about that, and God can help you, but you still have to deal with it head-on. Then, through prayer with God, you can begin to move towards a place of healing. When you are not healed, there are things that may come out of you. You may end up going off on people for no reason. An innocent person gets beaten up because you didn't give yourself time to heal and you could end up in conflict with them. You're sensitive, and you can easily take things overboard. Not being healed can cause you to be at odds with others.

What is the rush of trying to get over things so quickly? The truth is that you and I are moving on when we get up every day. We are taking time to grieve one step and one day at a time. That's why grief is a process of steps and actions you take, it's not a one and done move.

Again, time helps us to get over things. I want you to remember that time helps us to move. If you get that, you're going to be able to move. Every day when I get up, time helps me to move. Time heals as I go and helps me to keep going. Time helps me to go on and take just one more step, one more minute, one more second, one more hour, one more day. Start dealing with time.

My mother died in 2006. No one knew it, but I found myself thinking about her just the other evening. The tears started flowing. I'm not all the way there yet, but I'm better than I was. My uncle died in 2015, and here we are in 2022, and I'm emotional and still thinking about him. Why? Because moving on to another day doesn't mean you don't still grieve. It does mean you won't grieve as hard, nor as long. I say again, give yourself time to grieve. Give yourself time to heal and to get over some things. Don't rush it!

Some people don't go back to church for a while after the death of a loved one. I had a member whose brother committed suicide while he was in prison. I remember the day she called, and she was distraught and at work. My wife and I went to her, and we had to drive her home because she couldn't drive. They had the service for her brother, but it took her about two months before she could even come back to church. I called her one day, and I told her I was just checking on her. She just broke down crying. I said to her, I'm praying for you, and I will keep praying for you. Take your time. I need you to grieve like you need to and let God do what he needs to do. Then, when you're ready, you will come back". She took that time and she gradually started coming back to church. Then, eventually, she was back full time. What if I had been one of those who asked her why she was still crying? What if I told her she needs to get over it because two months have gone by?

That's insensitive, especially when you haven't been through that, and even if you have, you don't know what it is like for that person who is grieving.

My wife lost her sister LaShun in March 2022. Her sister Duranice passed January 2021, and she lost her mom, Mother Pace in July 2020. I told her that she needed to give herself time to grieve. My responsibility as a husband is to understand and not be insensitive during her grieving process. We must learn to not be insensitive during someone's grieving process and say insensitive things because that would hurt those who are grieving even more.

Learn to be a person that can be sensitive to the process of others by watching what you say and how you act. If you can't be sensitive, don't insert yourself in their process. We need to be careful not to say the wrong things or make comments at the wrong time. Concerning my wife, I am sensitive to her during this grieving process. What helps her is frequent visits with her sisters even in this pandemic. This helps her through her grieving process, and I understand it. Lady Martin and her sisters are doing okay, the best that they can. They've got to deal with these losses, and it may take a while. Even though they are sisters, they don't grieve the same way. **No one grieves the same way**. Don't let anybody fool you. My advice to everybody that is experiencing something like this is to trust God as you take your time to grieve. Don't let people push you or hurry your process.

Don't let people make you feel bad because you're

crying. You're supposed to get it out. Let the tears flow and the sorrow pass through you. Time takes care of some things. To give yourself some time, you don't have to shut yourself off. You don't have to avoid all fellowship and not talk to people. I'm not saying to become inactive or isolated but give yourself time to deal with the reality of whatever has happened.

You may need some help to deal with these things. Get help. Talk to God in prayer and talk with a Christian counselor, someone who is trained in this kind of process. There is nothing wrong with getting help to heal so you can function as a better person. Please prioritize getting help.

CHAPTER 5

NO ONE GRIEVES
THE SAME WAY

Recently, the United States reached a milestone with 986,319 deaths from the Coronavirus, a pandemic that hit us over two years ago. Since March 15, 2020, we were out of church for a year, and many churches were closed, but we are now back to having in-person worship. I've lost some friends to COVID-19. I was sick with it, in the hospital, and I almost thought I wouldn't come out of there. Thanks be to God that I came out! Again, I'm so grateful for that.

We've lost many people, not only from this virus, by many forms of death. As a result, countless numbers of people are dealing with grief. It's important for us to understand that there is no specific design, method, or pattern on how to grieve. Again, no one grieves the same way. There may be some people who say you don't need to grieve. However, I say, take your time to deal with your loss. When you can express your grief, you can move toward healing from grief, in your unique grieving process.

Before the pandemic, if someone were sick, visitors could be in the hospital room with them, could hold their hand

and care for them and talk to them, whether they were conscious or unconscious. At that time, it was possible to have the funeral of your loved one, and people would come from all over the world to honor and celebrate that life. When the pandemic started, much of that closure process was gone, but now we are starting to get back to having that type of closure. So much changed within that year. What a tragedy for those who have lived their lives well, deserving of honor and celebration from family, ministries, peers, and friends. Sadly, at the time that they should have been celebrated, some of them didn't even have a service, some only a graveyard service, a memorial service, or something totally different.

We've seen so much change and its effect on people dealing with grief. In August 2020, when I was admitted to the hospital, as I mentioned before, a friend of mine passed away that same day. I admit that every day since that time, I've thought about that particular day. That week was a hard week in my life as I dealt with my friend's sudden death and was struggling for my own life. I also had just buried my mother-in- law, Mother Bettie Pace, a few weeks before then. It had been over a month since my sister Duranice Pace had passed, and literally not long after that we lost my sister, LaShun Pace, suddenly. The grieving process for our family has been interrupted by one new death after another within the last couple of years. Because of what's happening in my life and the lives of our family, I'm a witness that no one grieves the same way and it's been hard.

Some people in the grieving process will disappear on you, and you can't find them. They don't want to be bothered by anybody. They don't want to talk to anybody. Then, there are others, while in the midst of their grieving process, who keep busy to deal with their loss and grief. I've noticed that my wife, Lady Martin, had not been going out much during the pandemic. Instead, she was content during the lock down to stay in the house. Again, since her sister Duranice passed, she's going out to spend time with her sisters, and they're talking every day. That is one of her ways of grieving.

A person grieving may do many different or new things in their process. The other day my wife and I laughed when her package of DVDs arrived in the mail. I asked, "What is this?" I know she loves those old movies, black and white movies, and musicals. I asked her, "Are you buying DVDs now?" She said, "Well, you know ever since my sister passed, I don't know, I just started buying DVDs." Some people deal with their grieving by shopping, and they purchase a lot of things. Others deal with it by eating, even if they are not hungry. One of the popular ways that helps others in the process of grieving is to post a lot of pictures of their loved ones on social media. Doing this is a way of remembering, and it's a way of showing love. It's a way of showing the pain of loss and respect to that individual that has passed away. That's natural, and they may be doing that the rest of their lives by recalling and sharing the special occasions they cherished. Some who are dealing with grief will go to the gravesite and cry. Some people will do things that remind them of their loved ones. I've noticed after Duranice passed that one of our family members listens to her music a lot and plays her DVDs or watches her on YouTube. You know, we go to the funeral service and see them close that casket and we go to the committal and watch them lower the body into the vault and seal it. It's so final on this earth. So FINAL!! Grief is a natural, human expression. Some of people's coping strategies may not seem to be the best strategies to people who are observing, but each person must grieve in the way that works for them. It may be difficult for you, who aren't grieving, to understand. Grieve your way. There are professional therapists who may share with you some methods and ways to grieve, but even when given professional advice, it is important to grieve your own way. It's ok to get the professional help we need. We need people to help us to walk through the process sometimes.

People have asked if we should grieve at all as believers? Yes, we should. It is the start of your healing. Grieving starts your healing process. It starts your journey to being and becoming better. You go ahead and grieve. Keeping it all in doesn't help. Letting out the pain and finding healthy expressions of grief are what allows the healing. Someone asked me if grieving takes away from being spiritual? No, it does not! It's human and expected. Even Jesus grieved. He was in human form. Grieving is not a thing that takes away from you being spiritual. I think that one of our greatest mistakes is trying to spiritualize everything. You can be as spiritual as you want to be, but if you get cut, you bleed because you're human. If you fall, you may break something, and that's human. Being spiritual, fasting, and praying doesn't stop you from having human experiences. When we start dealing with grief, the loss of a loved one, or whatever the source of the pain may be, you've got to give yourself time to deal with it from your human perspective. Don't let anyone make you feel bad if you want to get counseling to deal with your grief. There are professional counselors in church who are saved, and they have chosen the profession of helping people through difficult times.

You may be wondering how long you should grieve? You can't set a time frame for it. There is no expiration date on grieving. Sometimes you'll be doing fine. Sometimes you think you have gotten past a certain point. You think you're great. Then, suddenly, out of nowhere, you have one of those days or one of those moments that you break down crying like a baby. Some word, event, fragrance, or a song can shift your focus. Jamie Fox did a song in which he wrote a letter to his mother and grandmother. The lyrics of the song say, "I wish you were here to see what I've done." As I started playing that song, I heard the message, and the floodgates opened as I had thoughts of my mother, my uncle and grandmother. My mother and uncle were my biggest cheerleaders. They made me believe that there was nothing I couldn't do. If there was an event going on at my mother's church, and she had to have a speaker, you can rest assured I would be her choice. She would call me and tell me that she needed me to speak for her and to be her preacher. Every Sunday morning, she called me to check on me, and if I didn't pick up, she would say, "Hey, I was calling to check and see how you are doing this morning." That was the routine every Sunday morning. My uncle called me every November 23rd and no matter where he was in the country or the world, he called me to wish me a happy birthday. My mother passed away in 2006, and my uncle passed in 2015, but out of nowhere, the reality of their absence hits me from time to time. My grandmother died in 1976, over 40 years ago. We used to have a prayer meeting every Wednesday when she was living. The other day, I was going through old cassette tapes, and I found one with my grandmother's name on it, so I started playing it. The tape was of my grandmother and events surrounding when she got sick and came out of the hospital. This period was in the last six months of her life. She was talking on this tape about my uncle Gene's camp meeting, and how we were going to help him out. Listening to this and hearing her voice, I started to cry like a baby. You will experience times like that too.

Remember this please: It takes time for some things to heal, but don't ever think you will totally get over losing your loved one. Grief heals in time, and you will be strong enough to move on, and not be stuck. You learn to cope with it.

The church must do a better job when it comes to

helping people in the grieving process, especially considering these last few years, which have been such tough ones. We as the church haven't done a good job of telling people it's okay to grieve. To be fair, sometimes it's not that people are insensitive, but some people don't get it because they have never experienced loss and pain in that way. They have no sense of what it is like, so they don't get it.

Those of us that have been without our loved ones understand what it means to be without. When we see people that are without their loved ones, we have compassion because we've been there. We know what it feels like. Well, a person that's never been there doesn't know how to have compassion. I remember when the Coronavirus first hit, so many people were dying from COVID-19. Some were saying this was the judgment of God. They said that God was trying to get the church's attention. I noticed their tone changed when COVID-19 hit their house or their loved ones. Well, why did their tone change? Certainly, if God was judging everyone else, then what He was doing at their house was the same thing. When it hit their house, they felt no need to explain what was happening.

Now as I observe different ones in their grieving process, it is a process that I understand. I decided to talk about it. I was recently reminded by a text saying, "Thank you for Monday nights. Thank you for coming on and sharing with us because it's helping me and I needed to hear this conversation. I needed to know that some other people have gone through this also." You need to see somebody that you know, go through this process. Understand that it's okay to go through it.

Here is what I know and practice from years of dealing with death: Don't take it for granted that we will be here tomorrow. We are losing the old and the young today in vast numbers. Some people nowadays don't even live to the age of 50. I know at least four people a day that are asking for prayer, saying they have lost a loved one. We must pray for one another. Let's love each other while we have each other. Please don't take it for granted that I'll be here tomorrow, you'll be here tomorrow, or somebody else will be here tomorrow. If someone comes across your mind, and you can take an opportunity to speak with them, do it. When you do, say something kind and nice. By all means, let them know that you love them. Let's not continue to hold grudges and issues against one another. Time is too short. Life is too short for us to keep holding on to grudges and foolishness. We just got to let it go. Again, we must love each other while we have each other. I believe if we do that, we'll be fine!

52

CHAPTER 6

MONITOR YOUR PROGRESS TOWARD YOUR HEALING

Let's talk about monitoring your progress. Your grieving, hurting and disappointment are a part of your process, and you must monitor your progress on your way to your healing. When I was in the hospital in August 2020, I noticed some actions and steps that the staff of nurses and doctors did and continued until the last day I was there. When I first went in, they immediately hooked me up to a lot of machines. Before they even placed me in a room, they started an IV. Then, they put patches on my chest and hooked me up to a machine to monitor my heart. They put something on my finger to monitor my oxygen levels and pulse. This means that all vital functions, such as blood pressure, heart rate, breathing, and oxygen were being monitored. I couldn't read that information that the monitors were reporting. I had no clue what the numbers meant. All I knew was they were able to keep track of my body's functions, not just in the room, but even from a distance. They were monitoring my progress. They kept watching to see how I was doing. I clearly remember the last night I was there. About 2:30 in the morning, the nurse came into the room, and she said, "Uh, Mr. Martin, Mr. Martin." I answered her as she was talking on a walkie talkie. The person on the other end asked her, "Do you see him?" She said, "Yeah, he's here." I was trying to figure out what was going on. What happened was that the connection between the monitors for my heart on my chest and on my finger had gone out. I don't know if they thought that I was dead. I heard her say, "We see him. Now it is working." They were monitoring me. Because of their observations and keeping an eye on me, even when the monitors stopped working, they could tell something was wrong.

Sometimes when we go to the hospital or a doctor, they like to monitor us even after we've been dismissed and released. They tell us to come back as a follow-up so that our progress can be monitored. Even though you're out of the hospital, and you may feel better, it does not mean that you are completely healed. For the same reasons, I suggest that we need to monitor our progress toward our healing. When you're grieving, you need to monitor your progress. Understand that just because you feel better, doesn't always mean you're healed.

You can physically look better and still not be healed from the grieving process. Sometimes, you look better on the outside than you really are on the inside! We must be honest when we monitor our progress. Sometimes you must tell yourself that you're not better and that you're still dealing with grief. When you monitor your progress, you can know when you are finally OK. We sometimes allow people to push us into a position where we're not being honest about what we're facing. We're not being honest about what's happening. If you go to the doctor and are asked how you are doing, you're not going to tell them you're in pain because you don't want them to put you back in the hospital.

Other people may try to monitor your progress. They may give you more medicine. You'll tell them that you're okay and then go back home and try to deal with the pain yourself.

You must be honest to get well. We must be honest with ourselves and say, "I'm not having a good day. This is one of those days." There is nothing wrong with that. I know people can make you feel that something's wrong with that, or that you are weak. No, that is not so. You are human. You are having a bad day today, but that doesn't mean you will have such days every day. Monitor your progress to acknowledge that you are still grieving. You are still hurting. You are better than you were before, but if not properly attended to, you could end up being bitter instead of getting better. You could become bitter toward life and things that have affected you. You could also become bitter toward people, and it will come out when you least expect it.

Today, make up your mind that you are not going to stop monitoring your progress. It's important for you to see how far you've gotten. You will know that you are better when you can look at things and they don't affect you the way that they used to. In fact, they may still affect you some, but just not as much as they did in the past.

You can't allow others to push you into rushing the process. You are not crazy because you're doing this. That's why I don't criticize people who have had a devastating experience with grief.

Sometimes you see them posting pictures and videos. That is a way of healing and progressing.

That's a way of monitoring where they ask you how you're doing and how you're progressing. YOU have to see where YOU are. Consider the questions below:

- How am I dealing with what has happened?

- Where am I in this process?

- Am I still grieving?

- Does it still feel like it just happened?

- Is grief still taking hold of me and controlling me?

- Am I moving into an area of depression?

- Am I moving out of depression?

- Do I need to monitor this circumstance?

- Am I becoming isolated or more secluded?

- How am I interacting with people?

- Am I in a place where I don't want to be bothered with people?

- How close am I to being healed?

- Do I need help in this process?

If you don't monitor yourself, it's good to have people you trust to help you. As mentioned before, my wife is going through the grieving process right now. I'm being supportive and more sensitive to her grieving. I help her out and check in with her on several levels to see if she's okay. That's what we have to do with one another, whether family, friends, or loved ones. It's important that you have somebody that you can touch and connect with you, using compassion and honesty. Sometimes you need someone to listen to you. You just need to be able to talk. Occasionally, you will need to know someone is there for you. You are not alone. If you do that, you'll be fine. Allow them to check on you and let them help you. It's important to have a support system of people who won't judge you. There are people that can tell you beneficial things because of their own experiences. I have friends who have lost loved ones. I'm very supportive of and concerned for them. At times I can give them what I call tough love, trying to push them past a particular place that they are in. It's so easy to get stuck, and you will need someone to help you move further. Monitor your progress.

I don't think people understand the weight that comes with grieving, and how that weight can hold you down. In one case, Job 22:55 says, "My stroke is heavier than my groaning." Sometimes I can put on a mask. On the outside, everything looks okay, but if I am grieving, and I have on this mask, you can't see underneath it. Today we are wearing masks during this pandemic. With a mask on you really can't tell if I am smiling or frowning until I remove the mask. Many of us have masks on while we are grieving, and people don't see or understand the weight of the hurt, the weight of the disappointment, or the weight of the grief. That's why you have to monitor yourself. Say to yourself, "I can't wear the mask forever. I have to get better. When I do smile, I'm not just pushing a smile. I'm not smiling to keep from hiding and covering my hurt, but I'm smiling from a place that I'm getting better. Even though it may be hard, but I'm smiling a little more every day."

My nephew who recently lost his mother called me, and the conversation was about monitoring and helping him. He said, "I just need to talk to you. I know you know how it feels to lose a mother. I just need you to talk to me…. Do these things get better?" I said to him, "Yes, it gets better, but it's only with time. Right now, you're in the right place because you're supposed to feel what you're feeling. Don't let anybody tell you that you're not supposed to feel that. I don't care how saved you are and how filled with the Holy Ghost you are, you're supposed to feel that loss. You will feel her absence and you will miss her. You just lost your mother."

My grandmother died December 7, 1976. When she died, I was in the 10th grade on my way to ROTC, and while I was getting ready in the restroom, I heard a loud noise. I came out, and she was lying halfway off the bed. I called out to my aunt, telling her grandmother fell out the bed. We got her back up in the bed, and I was holding her. She took her last breath while I was holding her in my arms. There I was, and I had just turned 16 years old, and she took her last breath while I was holding her in my arms.

I left the house to pick up my aunt, and we saw the ambulance pass us. We thought it was taking my grandmother to the hospital. In that day, we didn't have cell phones. When we got back to the house, the medical team was bringing her out of the house. I was playing a song in the car. It was Walter Hawkins' song with Tremaine Hawkins singing "A Wonderful Change Has Come Over Me." I will never forget that day. Recently, some 40 years later, I was playing that song on a Sunday morning in my car, and it took me back to that Sunday morning, December 7, 1976. Yes, though I'm better than I was then, every time I hear that song, it takes me back to 40 years ago. I know I'm getting better when I am able to do things I could not do at first. I can pick up the belongings of the person that I lost and not feel as much hurt, or I can listen to their tapes and hear them sing without falling apart as much. It's truly a process. I'm getting to a better place, although I still miss them. You know what, you will get better too. Everyone's in a rush to get healed, but healing demands time. You have to be careful with that and monitor where you are. Be honest with yourself and deal with where you are. You don't ever want to get to the place where you are angry with God and everybody else too [See chapter 8, "DON'T LET YOUR GRIEVING TURN INTO ANGER"]. In that place you do things that you might later regret or realize you went way too far. You might say, "Lord I didn't mean to do that. That's not my character. That's not the way I am." When grief, anger, hurt, and disappointment are truly what you feel, you still need to

59

function with a level head. When you're angry, you don't function from a level-headed place. I try not to do anything when I'm angry. Even when my kids were coming up, I tried not to discipline them while I was angry. When you're angry, you may feel like punching holes in the wall, but don't do it. If you do, you will have to fix everything you break or replace what you have messed up, including other people's feelings. What is the sense of all that? That's why we must monitor our progress. At some point, you will see that you're better today than you were last week and better than you were two months ago. Please monitor your progress, and, say to yourself, "I need to make sure that I'm better." If you have good friends that you trust, let them talk to you and support you. Let them help monitor your progress.

Ask God to do something for you. Ask Him to touch and heal you. We need to let Him do it in His way and in His time, without rushing it. Again, don't let anybody rush you. Allow yourself to get to the place where the pain is not as great and the place where you are becoming stronger, healing, and getting better. Monitor your own progress.

CHAPTER 7

LEARNING HOW TO ADJUST

During the grieving process, you must learn how to adjust. It is a very important lesson that most of us will learn after losing a loved one. Adjusting is not always easy. It's not always fun. It's not always something that you want to do. Sometimes, it's not something you can do alone. The apostle Paul says, "Not that I speak in respect of want, for I have learned in whatever state I am in, to be content" (Philippians 4:11). He says to us that we may never be satisfied with where we are, but we've got to learn to make those adjustments in life so we can be content.

Life itself is full of adjustments. Every one of us will deal with it at various points in our lives. Adjustments take place in our personal lives, church, the workplace, etc. I don't know anyone who has not had to adjust. You can't get around it. I don't care who you are, how much we go to church, how much power we say we have, or how much Holy Ghost we have, we cannot get around adjusting. It is a part of life every day, especially while we're dealing with the grieving process.

If a wife loses her husband suddenly, and she was not

expecting to lose him, such as in the case of a heart attack, she has to adjust. A husband that loses his wife has to adjust. Family members have to adjust. Sisters and brothers have to adjust. Children have to adjust when parents die. Think about it, if you lose your mother, you must make an adjustment when Mother's Day arrives. If you lose your father, you must learn how to adjust on Father's Day. Adjustments are needed mentally, physically, and emotionally.

What do I mean? Well, you now have to move from the place of always seeing them or hearing their voice and them doing the things that you were accustomed to them doing. Mentally, you have to adjust. You will not see your loved ones anymore. You won't hear them talking anymore. You won't be on the phone with them, and they're not cooking special meals anymore. When you go into that area where they once lived, you can't go by to visit because they're not there anymore. When the holidays come, it is especially difficult. As mentioned before, you've got to deal even with the aftermath of cleaning out the room, cleaning out clothes, and the like. That's a significant physical adjustment that you have to make. Here's an example of how I began making adjustments after the loss of loved ones. About a day or two after they have transitioned, I normally delete their number out of my phone. The reason I do that is that I don't want to set myself up to dial their number or text them because it's a habit. Sometimes, when it's a habit and your routine to contact them, you have to learn to break that habit. If you don't do that, you'll find yourself picking up the phone to make the call. I remember doing this about three years ago. I had taken my uncle's number out of my phone when he passed. It was the number that we used personally for family. He always called me on that number. One day, I got a phone call from that familiar number, and I wondered who was calling. When I answered the phone, there was a young lady on the other end. She asked me if I was Dennis Martin, and I told her that I was. She said that she was calling me because somebody gave her my number. She said, "Evidently, this number that I have used to be your uncle's number, but this is my number now. People call me and ask to speak to him all the time". She said that everyone who has called and asked for him has had great things to say about him. She said that she had to tell them that it was no longer his number. When she said that, she invited me to Augusta, Georgia to one of the colleges to talk about my uncle on the topic of Black History.

A friend passed recently, and I had not taken his number out of my phone because I've been busy doing many other things. Today, I was watching the memorial service for him. I decided while I was watching that service that I needed to take his number out of my phone. I took it out and deleted it right then. It's important to make this adjustment to break the habit of going to our phones and calling the ones who are no longer here. We also need to consider removing the clothes and other things of our dearly departed. People tend to hold onto their loved ones' things and get stuck in the process of grieving because they won't adjust. They leave their loved ones' things in the closet, or they leave things just the way they were before their loved ones passed. They didn't adjust anything. They didn't move anything. Things are still there just as if the person is still there. We have to learn to adjust, so that we can begin to heal.

Adjusting helps us heal. We must do that. I know we don't hear that a lot. People don't talk about that in church or other places where you might expect to get help. Making these adjustments will be a blessing to you and bring you closer to where you need to be in your healing process. Not making proper adjustments can affect you physically. Sometimes we grieve so hard that our bodies physically start reacting to it in a negative way. Disappointments and hurt do affect us.

Even though I understand that it's important not to rush the matter of adjustments, it's also important to start adjusting as much as possible. Delay can affect you physically. It can get you into a state of depression, where you don't want to eat, and you don't want to do anything. You don't want to talk to anybody. You don't want to be bothered. The truth is that if we're going to come through grief and come out of it, we all must adjust. When I dealt with my sickness with COVID-19, I was in the hospital for ten days, and I lost 20 pounds. When I came out, I had to wear a different set of clothes. My daughter and my wife had to buy me some new clothes to wear because I couldn't wear my old clothes. I went to church and put on a robe, and the robe was too big for me.

Then, I put on my suits, and my suits were too big for me. One day the electrician was working at our house, and he was talking about how he had lost weight and he told me about a person that can adjust my clothes. We called him up and I took him my suits for alteration. Now those suits fit like a glove. That's an adjustment I had to make. **I had to alter what I have to make it work for where I am.** That is a lesson. Paul said, "I've learned that whatsoever state I'm in" (to be content). It's not something that you automatically do. He said, I've got to learn how to do it. It wasn't something that just naturally came. As we begin to learn to adjust, what we'll find and see is that things are better and we're getting better, with each adjustment. That's important.

Learning how to adjust is uncomfortable. Sometimes adjustments can hurt, but adjustment is necessary to get to your next destination, the place that God has for you, a place of victory.

We must make the adjustments that are necessary to get to the next place. For example, you must learn how to adjust if there's a roadblock. The construction crew gives you a detour sign and route. You have to learn to follow the signs so you will get back on the right road to your destination. Learn to adjust. Don't beat yourself up and go through unhealthy changes about necessary adjustments. We've lost loved ones. We've got hurts and disappointments. Learn to adjust so you can live. When you learn them through prayer, and even through fasting, I guarantee you that you will come out alright every time. Adjustments are not as bad as you think they are.

CHAPTER 8

DON'T LET YOUR GRIEVING
TURN INTO ANGER

Don't let your grieving turn into anger. The challenge for us is to go through the grieving process and not to get stuck in grief. If there's a loss of a loved one or something that happens to us that affects us emotionally, it hits us. There may be anger about what has happened. The challenge is not to avoid getting angry but when we become angry, don't settle there. Move from there to a healed place.

There are a lot of people right now that must deal with grief as we go through the process of death, loss, and devastation. I want to talk to you from the other side. Don't allow your grief to turn into anger. I want you to know that there is a thin line between grieving, getting angry, and it can turn into bitter anger. It is possible for you to move from that place of grieving to healing, or you can fall into another deeper place suddenly, a place of intense anger, and not even know that you've crossed the line into that place. You still think you're just grieving, but it's beyond grieving. By then, it has become a constant bitter anger that you now embrace. There is, again, a thin line before a person crosses into that place.

I'm going to share some of the things that can happen as you go into that place. As you slip over into that state, which results when you stay in grief rather than dealing with the process, you can go into a place which I will call the dark place. You know you are there when you have transferred your hurt over to deep anger in that dark place. You are not still grieving, but your anger has taken over the grieving process. I want to just share with you some things that sort of let you know that you have moved over into that place. I've talked with people who have been grieving. As a pastor, I've talked with people who have lost loved ones, including siblings, children, and parents. Sometimes they were untimely deaths, and others were expected passings. Then, I've talked to others with whom death wasn't involved at all in the issues of grieving. This was just a matter of dealing with some other forms of losses, such as a certain status, specific influences, a relationship, or other losses that might leave someone hurting deeply. No matter what the case was, they've had to deal with grieving, and they became angry.

I want to tell you that sometimes when we move from grieving into anger, we completely ignore it! Those of us who are believers will generally get angry with God. Now I know that someone is going to say, "Not me," but it is a fact that people often get angry with God. There are people who even say, "I am angry with God because I don't understand why God allowed this to happen. I don't understand why God did this, why He didn't stop it. Why didn't He intervene? Why didn't He do this or why didn't He do that?" They get angry with God. That's why sometimes they'll say, "I'm not praying anymore. I'm not going to church anymore. I'm not doing this. I'm not doing that". Why? Because now they are angry with God. You may just say that you're still grieving, but that anger has taken over and slowly moves you to be angry with God. You're upset with God for the mere fact that you feel God did not do what you thought He should have done. I've talked to people who would say, "I need you to pray for me". I would tell them, "Well, I'm praying for you". Then, they would say, "No, you don't understand, I'm upset." If asked who they are upset with, they say, "I'm angry with God. I'm upset with God because God didn't do what I thought He should have done". It is so possible for us to smoothly switch over into that place where there's a seething anger against God. Your desire to be connected to God is severed by deep anger.

In that dark place you don't pray anymore, or you don't see the need to talk to God, and you despise it when people start telling you about things of God like reminding you that He loves and cares for you. Anytime someone tries to give us some understanding, we get angry. We resist, and we don't deal with the anger. We don't do well in such a dark place. I was talking with someone the other day and they were saying that because of them tuning into these discussions on my Monday Nights Live on Facebook, they were able to share with an elderly gentleman that had lost his young son to cancer. This elderly gentleman was a Deacon in the church, but he was having a hard time going back to church. He had a hard time doing things because he was grieving the loss of his son. Then, he didn't understand why God allowed his son to die at such an early age with cancer. However, after sharing with the elderly Deacon some of the things that I had been teaching, we are glad to report that he started coming around. He now understands how he had gotten into anger and how he now knows he needs to return to God. Please understand this can happen to anyone, where people get angry with God. If you don't allow yourself to let this process of grief get to the point of healing, anger will drive you from God. Be careful that you don't go over into the dark place where your grieving turns into constant anger. First, you're angry with God, then your grieving turns into anger with family and friends.

When I mention anger, I'm not saying that it is in a violent way, but you get angry, start lashing out, and start doing things against family and friends that you wouldn't ordinarily do because you are irritated, annoyed, hostile, vexed and bitter. You wouldn't do those things under normal circumstances, but a place of anger leads you to act in certain ways. Now, family and friends don't know how to say things to us or approach us. They're trying to figure out how to deal with us because it looks like no matter what is said, it triggers something in us. It triggers a negative reaction and a negative response. Those around us are struggling to know, "How do I deal with this person now?" The people who love you, who are concerned about you, and who want to help you as much as they can, should not be the victims of your lashing out. This happens though. We do that against family, and we do it against friends. When we go back to work, people just sort of stay away from our cubicle or work area because they don't know how to address us. Somebody can say hello to you, and that it's a good day, and the first thing you say is, "What's good about it?" Hey, they didn't mean any harm. But you see how quickly we can fall right over into hostility and not understand where we are and how long we've been there. In that anger, we go from grieving to insults and sarcasm, meanness toward the very people who love us. I mean, be honest, you know we do that, but we don't mean to do it. Sometimes, we must go back and apologize. Why? Because we act and respond out of anger and frustration. We just sort of snap at those around us. We must be careful that grieving doesn't turn into anger. When that happens, we start mishandling family, friends, people who love us, and people who care about us. There are times that we may need to sort out where our responses are coming from. Perhaps a moment is needed to step back from where people are. Perhaps you need a moment to get away. You need to recognize when you need a moment. You may need more than a moment. You may need some me-time, so you can make an adjustment and stop lashing out at others. It's ok to take that needed time to move past the anger and let healing come. Every one of us agrees that sometimes, we need some me-time. We go to the left, and don't even understand why we're going to the left. It's because we're on that borderline between

71

grieving and anger. Let's make sure we begin paying attention to that. Come away from the edge. Take time with God to release the anger. Monitor that place of anger with God, anger with family and friends. Be careful to monitor anger against yourself. While you are grieving, stop being angry at yourself. When you get angry at yourself, that's a whole different place you step into. When you're angry with yourself, it's different from being angry with family, friends, or co-workers. It takes on a whole different meaning. You're angry with yourself because you feel you didn't do enough. You start to blame yourself. When you start doing that, you must understand that's not a good place to be in when we're grieving. That place can become a dark place of depression, shame, and guilt. You know we don't like to talk about dark places, but it can become a dark place with thoughts of harming yourself. It's a vicious cycle. You are angry with yourself, you grow angrier with God, and angrier with others. Self-anger will open you up to all kinds of thoughts going through your mind, with dread in your head, and you must be careful.

During those times, you may prefer not to be around other people. So, when you are alone, in dangerous isolation, you talk anger, not against others, but you're talking against yourself. You doubt yourself. You don't see any positive thing in you. You become self-loathing. You don't see anything in you that's good. You focus on all your negative flaws, all your negative features. You point them out and start believing what everyone else has negatively said about you, but the fact is, at this point, you're moving from grieving to anger and then to a dangerous place. When you are upset with yourself, you have no peace, no rest, no joy. This is so dangerous because the cycle can go on for an extended period. This battling is a constant thing. This negativity is on your mind when you wake up. It's on your mind when you go to sleep. It's on your mind when you drive, and it's on your mind wherever you are. We must learn to monitor ourselves and not to allow ourselves to let these things slowly transition into anger. When you are just upset with yourself, you could end up doing something crazy. When I say crazy, I am not necessarily talking about suicide, but even trying to drown your pain in poor substitutes for health and healing, like wrong associations, and bad choices that have consequences that you will have to deal with down the road.

Sometimes we must get a resolve within ourselves to deal with and accept what is, but we can't allow our grieving to make us angry with ourselves, especially over some things we can't do anything about. There are many things we have no control over. Some things would have happened the way they did, even if we were present during the time that we lost our loved ones. You can only be responsible for what you can control. You don't control other people, circumstances, or God's will about death. What you must do is get up from where you are, and stop being angry at yourself. Stop being angry with God and others too. You have the power to make that choice. Choose acceptance over anger. Anger will take you where you don't want to go and it will hold you hostage, but God can help you to get back.

Moving from grieving to anger, you start doing things and saying things that sometimes you can't take back, and you can't resolve. You can't fix the situation, and you can't pull back what you have said and/or done. Maybe you are sorry about it, but some things you can't take back. Counselors will tell you when you're angry and upset that you should take a moment to calm down, chill, and if you need to, just leave the house. Right now, there are many people in jail today that are not murderers by nature. Many people in prison today are not killers, not by nature, but they're in prison simply because they got angry and could not control it and went too far. They did something that they regret for the rest of their life. Anger got the best of them. So that's why you must watch yourself as you're dealing with grieving. You must monitor yourself so that you don't develop anger and start doing things that you can't reverse, actions that you can't withdraw from, or make statements that create damage that can't be undone. As a parent, you can get angry with your children over something they do. You can say something that means nothing to you but can crush your children and follow them for the rest of their lives, simply because your anger got the best of you. Even though we apologize for it, there is still an imprint left. It could leave a scar for life. Why? Because we did not understand that in our anger, we can do harmful things. The scripture tells us that we can be angry, but sin not. There's a thin line for crossing over into that place of anger, and you can sin with your words and deeds. If someone triggers you, and you are staying in that constant angry place, we recommend getting professional help. You could have mental challenges and health issues, and you need to see a professional. Just coming to church, getting prayer, and going on may not be enough. I agree with prayer and its power, and I pray for many people, but there are times when people need professional help. Get some professional help. That's why we have saved, professional, Christian counselors.

You need to know what your trigger points are and how to manage them. We never know what may trigger people. Maybe something happened in their childhood. Sometimes, when people are bullied, they harm others simply because somebody pushed the triggers in them. They were bullied at some point in their past. Their resolve is to go after who they think is bullying them now. They get out and go on a shooting spree and change your life. A person could have those triggers and not know where or what they are, so they should seek help. A person could need more than prayer alone. If you are slipping over the edge into darkness, constant anger, hostility towards God, others, and yourself, you need to seek professional help. We all must be careful when we grieve to not let anger get the best of us. Grief counselors can help you monitor yourself too. If we see that we need help, we need to get it and stop acting like we don't need it.

You watch people, and you observe they are bent on

destroying everybody and destroying everything. They are obsessed with one thing. They may want to bring harm to themselves or others, they are vengeful, and they may verbalize that if it's the last thing they do, someone will pay. That person or those people are a danger to themselves and others. Grieving has turned into anger.

Sometimes a person may hurt you. All your time is spent trying to figure out how to get back at them. You may ask, "How can I destroy them?" You must be careful that you don't pursue and do that. That's why I often say in relationships, dating, and in marriage, that you must know who you are dealing with. Note that if someone is spending money on you, and you're dating and talking, he or she becomes possessive acting like they own you. They check on you with lots of calls and may question why you didn't pick up the phone and where were you when they were trying to reach you. That type of behavior is a red flag. Soon, he/she feels a certain kind of way. If you break off from this person, sometimes he/she doesn't know how to manage it and goes into the grieving and the relationship then slips into a dark angry place. Next thing you know, you are being stalked and you're trying to figure out what you did to get there. You didn't do anything, but that's just one of those triggers of rejection you pushed and didn't know it. He or she can drive by your house, and sees somebody else's car there, and before you know it, some disaster has occurred. You've heard incidents where an estranged partner killed the person that they once were dating.

In this day and time when a female gives herself to you, emotionally, mentally, and even physically, and she feels that you played with her emotions, and that you tried to hit it and quit it, things could escalate quickly in the wrong direction. She could get to the point that she feels if she can't have you, nobody will have you, and anger gets the best of her. Next thing you know, they don't hurt just the other individual, they could turn around and kill themselves over a relationship or something that didn't seem to work out. Why? Because that's the reality of anger. That's why we have to talk about things and learn anger management. We have to deal with anger because anger takes you to a place where you either cause harm to someone else or cause harm to yourself. When that has taken place, it's clear that you were not thinking in the moment. Then, later, you regret what you did. When we are blinded by anger, it blinds our thoughts and our judgment, and it overwhelms what we do. There's no telling what you're apt to do. You'll do things that you wouldn't normally do simply because now your judgment has been blinded by anger. It is critically important that we are careful that we don't allow our grieving to turn into anger.

Remember these important things that we must watch out for: First, it is important to look out for signs of being angry with God. Second, we must observe for signs of being angry with others, such as our family, our friends, even co-workers, and even saying things that we can't retract, or doing things that we can't take back. Third, look out for being angry with yourself. Lastly, anger can cause you to harm others and yourself. So be careful how you drift into anger. We have to have these honest conversations, not just designed to make people feel better and good. Sometimes we have these conversations that say, "Hey, this is where I am, this is where we are. I need help to come out of this place of anger".

CHAPTER 9

DON'T BLAME YOURSELF

Many people are grieving over things that have happened surrounding the death of family, loved ones and friends, but that grief is compounded with guilt. They're carrying around the weight of guilt mixed with grieving, because they're blaming themselves, and they continue to blame themselves for some things they could not control or change.

It is normal as we move through grief to deal with some sense of guilt or responsibility. Even when it doesn't make logical sense, almost everyone slips into "what if" scenarios, trying to figure out if there was anything we could have possibly done to extend the life or our loved one. They might ask, "What if I prayed more, believed harder, stayed by their side, made another call?", or any one of a thousand thoughts that could crowd the mind. When the reality of death sets in after the shock and denial of losing our loved one, this senseless reasoning hits hard and weighs heavy. The roller coaster ride begins, but it's by no means an enjoyable one. You deal with this day by day. There is shock and denial, pain and guilt, anger and bargaining, depression, acceptance, and finally, rebuilding your life as you move forward in this strange new normal, in the absence of the one who has passed away.

Guilt and blame are normal and typical emotions you find in the early stages of grief, but if you get stuck there, these can cause you to have physical challenges and changes. Your body reacts because of the stress you put on yourself while grieving, and things will happen to you physically. I want to say to you, please stop blaming yourself. Examine and look at where you are in this grieving process. What's currently happening to you? We must deal with these particular things and understand what is going on and how to move from under the weight and pressure of blame and guilt to live. Many people are dealing with guilt about things that took place that can't be changed, and they carry that guilt, not just for a day, or a month, but they carry it for years. They carry guilt for years just feeling bad and guilty about what has happened beyond their control. They bear that burden and beat themselves up. They are slowly crushed by that feeling because blame and guilt are not a manageable weight to carry in the heart or mind. I want to tell you to stop blaming yourself. Stop blaming yourself for things that you had no control over.

When you don't have control over a thing, you cannot blame yourself for how things turned out. When I say no control, you can't control it, and you have no control over it. You can't change it now and couldn't have changed it then.

Although things are starting to open back up during

this pandemic, initially, unless you were the patient, no one else was allowed in the hospital. When the pandemic struck, hospitals were closed to all relatives and visitors. When your loved ones went into the hospital, for any reason, surgery, COVID or other illnesses, you were not allowed to go into the hospital. That was something beyond your control.

I've talked to people whose loved ones have died during this pandemic with the Coronavirus and other medical issues. They couldn't even be in the room. They could only talk to them or see their last response through Zoom, FaceTime or whatever technology afforded them a final view. This was something that they couldn't control. If you were in one of those situations, you can't beat yourself up over something that you had no control over. You had no control over when or if you could go in and be with your loved one in their final hours. When I got COVID, my family had to drop me off at the front door of the hospital. Thank God that 10 days later, they were able to pick me up from the front door, but they had no control over the fact that they were not allowed in those doors to see me. They can't blame themselves for something that they had no control over. If something would have happened to me, they still should not have blamed themselves or questioned whether they could have done something differently. Honestly, even if they could have been there in the room, they couldn't have done much, but they were doing what they could while they were not there with me. That is, my family was praying. That was a good thing they could do. I came out because God heard the prayers.

Let me say to you that you've got to stop blaming yourself over something that you have no control over, whether it deals with someone that's passed on or someone that's even alive today. If you have no control over certain things, why blame yourself? Why carry that burden? Why carry that guilt? Why carry that weight? Why carry that and grow weak, sick, sad, and depressed? You are not responsible when you have no control over what's going on. Know that. Understand that. Stop beating yourself up or allowing others to dump this weight on you.

Relieve yourself. You are blaming yourself and your hands were tied! You had no control over the circumstances, the situation, or the outcome that was taking place! Don't buy into the guilt trip and blame game. Because of it, you're weighed down, and you're stressed out. You are not eating. You are not taking care of yourself. You are not doing the things you need to do. Bring this to an end! Stop blaming yourself!

Don't blame yourself for another person's actions. Everyone must take responsibility for their own actions. I think that's important for us to accept this before we go to blaming ourselves. Now, we know there are some situations where you must deal with people that may have Alzheimer's or some form of dementia, or mental illness, but that's a little different. However, people who are in their sound mind don't get to escape responsibility for their actions. You can't cover for them. You have to let people take responsibility and become accountable for their actions. You can't feel bad because they did something that you didn't have any control over, but they did it themselves. So, they must take responsibility for their own actions. You cannot feel guilty or blame yourself for the actions of grown people. I must say that, again, for somebody in the back of the room. You cannot feel guilt and blame yourself for the actions of grown people. People are grown. When people get into trouble, they want you to rescue them, but let grown folks be grown. They'll tell you in a minute, "I'm grown". When you're grown, you must take responsibility. Do not take yourself through changes because grown folks don't want to be accountable for what they did and should have known better. Really, a lot of parents and others were running around feeling guilty over somebody's actions that are grown. I mean, grown people do grown up stuff, and we can't beat ourselves up over what they're doing. I say to them, "So you are grown, or you feel like you are grown, then you have to take responsibility for your actions". We put ourselves in a bad place because we are trying our best to be responsible and feel guilty over what they did, and if we interfere, they will never take responsibility for the action themselves. I think that my kids have sound minds, but if they did something, I'm not going to try to explain to you why they did it. You need to talk to them. They are grown. Then, I'm not going to feel guilty, and neither will I let you lay their irresponsibility or things they did to my charge. That had nothing to do with me. You've got to stop letting people lay to your charge what your grown kids did or what they are doing. They are grown. They make their own choices in life. They do what they want to do with family and friends or whomever they choose. Personally, I'm not going to blame myself and be guilty of what somebody else is doing. It's not your responsibility to feel guilty either. We must stand and say, "I can help you, but I can't help you if you don't want to help yourself. Be responsible." That's what we got to deal with. If people don't want to help themselves, you are somewhat wasting your time because people have to want to help themselves. When you're dealing with grown folks, and I'll say that again, people have to take responsibility and be accountable for their actions. You can't live in a place of guilt over what grown people have done or are doing. Regardless of who they are, you can't do it. They're grown. They made a conscious decision, and they made a choice.

Years ago, Flip Wilson played a character named Geraldine. He would always say the devil made him do it when he did something inappropriate. Some of us say the devil made us do it, and that is our excuse, but you can't do that. You must take responsibility for your actions. If you are a caregiver, you help those out in your charge, but all my children are grown. They have to take responsibility for their actions. I can't feel guilty for what they do. I don't hold myself accountable for them. You have to stop blaming yourself and feeling guilty over your children and grown folks because some of you and some of us are going to feel better when we stop doing that!

Blaming yourself can make you feel like you are failing. You can't allow other people's actions to make you feel like you are a failure. You haven't failed. When you stop blaming yourself and saying, "Well, I probably could have done more...," Truth is that all of us could have done more. So that's not even a question. A lot of us could have done a whole lot of things. A pastor friend of mine posted something the other day, and we got a chance to talk about it and it's so true. He's younger than me. He was appointed at his church, and he said that if he could go back, there are some things he would handle differently. I agree. When I look at some things at my church, I would handle them differently, but at the same time, I'm not a failure. However, I can't go back and blame myself and feel like a failure. It serves no purpose and promotes no progress.

Even when you have instilled values and principles in your children, trained them, talked to them, and put what we think is the best before them, they can make some unwise choices. If they turn out to be criminals, then you shouldn't sit up and feel like you failed as a parent. Rehearsing in your mind this doom cycle, "Maybe if I did this, and perhaps if I did that...then I wonder if things would have been..." Stop it. You raised them and taught them; you are not a failed parent.

Listen, some people will do what they want to do, no matter how much conversation or how much talking you do with them or how much you share with them. They're going to do what they want to do and do it their way. When they do that, then you've got to stop saying, "Well, I don't know, maybe

I could have done this or that." No, it's probably not possible for you to do it differently now anyway, and that's just the way they chose to handle things. Blaming yourself and believing you are a failure is futile. You're not a failure because of other people's actions. What they choose to do is what they choose to do. I'm not a failure because of other people's actions. I'm not a failure because of my kid's actions or my friend's actions or my family's actions. They do what they do, and they're not responsible for my actions either.

You have to let that go. It is the way it is and stop going through changes about it. Blaming yourself can make you feel guilty, and then it can cause you some physical challenges because you're putting that weight and that pressure on yourself. It would help if you looked at that a little differently. Say this: "I must stop blaming myself. You can only do what you can do and do that well and right!

A primary point of my advice to stop blaming yourself is one for life: Do what you can do and don't worry about the rest. Do what you can do, only what has been afforded to you to do, and stop blaming yourself for what they did or did not do. You make yourself sick and hurt going through unnecessary changes. I've had a conversation with people trying to help them and I started understanding that I can't help everybody or change everything. You do what you can do. Then, you let them do what they can do. We try to work this out, but when I talk to you and try to help you, I'm not feeling guilty after that. I'm not going to beat myself up after that. I have a saying that I used to say all the time: "I promise you that I will not come back and throw it in your face and say I told you so." I try not to do that to people because they already feel bad about the issue anyway, but at the same time, I don't blame myself for what they did. I'm not doing that. That's just not going to happen. People have a way of using that reverse psychology when they know they didn't do their part and want to lay blame and guilt on you. Don't let them do it. They will turn things around and reverse them. They will have you feeling bad about something that they should take responsibility for themselves. You have people who are professionals at using reverse psychology. They do those things, knowing that they have you sitting there feeling guilty about something and trying to act like if you had done this, then it wouldn't be this way. They have no conviction and enjoy watching you suffer because of their irresponsibility. You must stop letting people do that. For example, instead of people apologizing to you, they say, "Well, if you hadn't said this, I wouldn't have said that, and every action brings on a reaction". That's not an apology! Just say you are sorry, and let's move on. Just say I'm sorry, and let's move the ball down the field. That's what we need to do instead of all this other stuff in the blame game. Please stop blaming yourself and stop beating yourself up. If you can get control over this, you will be much better.

Today the thing that is killing a whole lot of us is stress. I'm saying stress is killing us, and then the pandemic didn't help because we were locked down. Then we go to blaming and beating ourselves up. No wonder we are sick. I can't do it. Let me put it to you this way. If I am wrong, I will admit my part if I'm in error as it relates to you, me, our relationship. That's how we handle it. I admit my part. If I said something I shouldn't have said, I apologize. Forgive me. If I handled you in a way that I shouldn't have handled you, I'm going to apologize. I'm only going to deal with that. After that's over, I'm not going to blame myself. If you apologize to me, I accept the apology, then we will move on. Now, here's the thing. If I apologize to you, or you apologize to me, the next time something comes up, do not bring that back up as your sounding board. I forgave you last time as you did me. Why are you mentioning that? We already went past that point. You say you forgave me, and we talked about that. So why do you bring it up again? You can't open that conversation back up and drag this one into it. Why must we go back through this whole thing again? No, don't do that. There's that reverse psychology stuff, that stuff that makes you say let's learn to take responsibility on both sides.

Let's stop feeling guilty about stuff that we have tried to help people with. You can't blame yourself because you can't help them. For some people, it goes past grieving. It goes past blaming you. Some people love attention. They will never get to the place to get past certain things. I'm not talking about the grieving of a loved one. They'll never get past that either. Because if they get past it, then they won't get the attention that they want. They want your time and attention.

You see how we all must be accountable. You must stop

blaming yourself and stop letting people put you in that place where you feel guilty and bad. Don't carry stress in your life over stuff that you can't control. You can't do anything trying to help people that don't want any help. Finally, stop blaming yourself as a caregiver. Some of you were caregivers for your parents, a sibling, spouse, child or loved one. You did a great job! You were there. You took care of them. You spent your money providing for them, and you gave your time. You came from work and went straight to take care of them. It just so happened that they passed. It is something that you had no control over. You can't beat yourself up over the fact that they passed away. You did your best. Be consoled in the fact that you did your best. You took really good care of them.

Even if you have a sibling or somebody who's on drugs, and you try your best to help them out, and they just seem like they don't get better, don't beat yourself up over that. Keep praying for them. Keep trying to help them and keep praying for them, but don't feel guilty. Even if they don't receive help, you can still try, but don't beat yourself up and say, well, I don't know anything else I can do. You know, I did that. My uncle got sick and ended up in the hospital. Then, he ended up with my cousin Michelle and her husband, Johnny. Michelle was taking care of him. If she couldn't take him to the doctor, I would take him to the doctor. When he got sick and was in the hospital, I visited him every day. The week that he died, I was in Jacksonville, Florida, I preached, and I flew back home. I was going to see him the night I got back, but I was so tired, and I had another business meeting to attend, and I did not make it that day. When I got up the next day, and I was dropping my daughter off at church, she was getting ready to do a recording. My cousin called and said my uncle had just passed. I felt certain ways because I missed seeing him for the last time. I started saying I should have done this or that, and I should have pushed past my tiredness to get to him. The reality is that it was the Lord's will. There wasn't anything I was going to be able to do about preventing him from his transition anyway. In time, I learned that I can't blame myself for that.

The same thing happened with my mother. I went to preach, and usually, my revivals end on Friday, but I had scheduled it to end on Thursday night, and I went home Friday. I talked to my mother before I left. I said to her that I would be flying out the next day. I told her that I wouldn't get to her that day, but I would see her when I got back. I was intending to visit her when I got back to the house where she was staying. Friday, I had an early flight and I got back. I was very exhausted, so I went home to lay down and take a nap for a few hours. When I got up and went to see my mother, my brother, Cedric, met me at the door and told me that they had just taken her away. I didn't know exactly what he meant. Then, he told me mom had passed. What I felt in that moment and for a while was guilt and blame. What if I had pressed to see her, but I was so exhausted that I couldn't. The what ifs kept playing in my head and breaking my heart, but I learned to let it go and stop blaming myself.

I'm saying to you that if you have taken care of your loved ones while they lived, and if you have done all you could do, if you pressed to make good things happen for them, don't blame yourself. Just thank God for the opportunity you had to do what you could do for them while they lived. I get the joy of knowing that when my mother lived and she got ready to go on a trip, I could go by and give her money to make it nicer. Sometimes, I was on my way out the door, and about to get in my car, the Lord told me to go back and give her some more money. I went back and gave her more money. She said to me, "Well, I know you hear from God". What a memory to have of my mother to hear her say, "I know you hear from God" and give her a bright moment.

I relieved her and found relief in the things I did to make her happy. Before she died, I was made the International President of Evangelism for the Church of God in Christ. She was so happy and proud. I have experienced the same thing with my uncle and other loved ones.

We should have no regrets. Don't blame yourself! Don't let anybody blame you and make you feel bad. Let your testimony be, "I gave it my best. There were those that I tried to help, and they just didn't want it. There's nothing I can do about that either. I did my best and I'm going to live knowing this truth".

I pray and trust that this has helped those who have been living with this distress, this burden, this guilt of blaming yourself. Be lifted and be free!! Elder Albert Pass from Holly

Springs, Mississippi always says, "When you've done your best, the angels in heaven can't do any better. You did your best". I want you just to remember that. You did what you did. You did a good job!

CHAPTER 10

THE WORST THING YOU CAN SAY WHEN PEOPLE ARE GRIEVING

So many people have lost their parents, spouses, siblings, children, and friends. Not just older people, but also younger people are passing away. When people are grieving, there are things we should never say or do. Whether they're grieving from losing a loved one, grieving from disappointments, hurt, other losses or whatever it may be, we should not be insensitive. Sometimes, those of us who have never experienced grief in a certain way tend to be insensitive in dealing with those who are grieving.

If you cannot understand why someone has been grieving for so long, consider yourself fortunate that you do not understand it. That probably means you haven't experienced grief on that level. Sometimes, it takes a while to deal with what just happened or the things that just took place. If you haven't been in such a place, you probably won't understand it. You can lose someone that may not be as close to you and deal with grief differently than when you lose someone very close to you. I hope this helps us all to understand that some things are not good to do or say when people are grieving. **First, if you don't know**

what to say, it's best NOT TO SAY ANYTHING AT ALL.
When people are grieving, one of the things they need the most from us is a listening ear, not always talking. Sometimes they need us to be quiet and just listen. They do not need our input or a word of encouragement. We are needed to listen to them so they can sort things out, share their hearts, and perhaps lighten the load of the things they're facing and dealing with. Don't try to be super spiritual and say something that you think sounds profound. When grieving, people don't need that. They just need you to be quiet and listen even if when they talk, it sounds like they are rambling to you. It's not rambling. It's them trying to grasp and process it all. But you want to talk, and that's not the time. If you want to say something to connect, then every now and then say," uh- huh", "I understand", or "I'm praying for you." Remember they need you to listen, to tell you how they feel, to try to explain what this feels like for them and how it affects them. We've got to learn that sometimes it is not always good to talk, and, in these cases, it is better to listen.

There are times I've heard people say, "Well, you know, you need to get over it." That's the worst thing you can say to a grieving person!!! Do not tell them, "You just need to get up, get over it and move on." It's easy for you to say that when you're not in that place. It's easy for you to say that when you're not dealing with what they are dealing with. Not everyone will get over loss at a certain point in time, although we pray everyone comes through the grieving process. We pray that they get to the extent of handling the losses and can move forward, but this doesn't mean that they will get over it right away, especially if it's fresh. It may take a month, two months, three months, sometimes longer than that, and the grief is still fresh. It takes time. For you, for me or anybody else to be insensitive, and say to them, "You need to get over it", is not good. YOU need to be quiet. Any person who does this is an insensitive individual. I know people who are still dealing with grief years after their loss. When I speak with them, I try to encourage them to move forward, do things, and live. Still, I've never expressed to them that they should just get over it and move on. You have to choose your words carefully so that you don't say the wrong words to those who are grieving. Some people are going to flip out and go to the left on you. You're going to wonder why they are acting like that. Well, they are wondering why you had to say what you did. YOU said the wrong thing. You went to the wrong area, and you shouldn't have said that. You should have just kept your mouth closed, and everything would have been fine, but no, you decided that you were going to open your mouth and say the wrong things.

Therefore, it is important to know what to say and what not to say. Here is another bit of wisdom: When you are talking, you should not mention negative things when people are grieving about their loved ones. So, what if the person who passed was not all you thought they should have been, whatever their lifestyle was? This person matters to the one that is grieving. They may not have been anything to you, but they are something to somebody. So don't say unkind things. That's wrong. There are things that you shouldn't say at all if it's not uplifting. Then, when the person who is grieving checks you, it's because you started it with the wrong words. Listen, if you don't like a thing, if you don't agree with something, just leave it alone. If you don't have anything good to say, please go on your way and do what you do. Leave them alone. We are losing too many people for us not to be sensitive to others who are grieving.

You know, most times when people pass away, we want to know what they died from right away, but to the family that's a frustration most times to repeat over and over the cause of death or even to have that conversation immediately with other people is an undue burden. Be sensitive. In the list of what not to say and to leave alone, please stop making your main concern what condition or circumstances caused the deceased one's death. **Make your main concern for the living and the grieving.** Your first statement should be, "I'm praying for you" and not, "What was the cause of death?" Yes, it's human to be concerned, but if the person that's grieving doesn't bring it up, leave it alone. Don't badger them with questions. If they want you to know, it may come up in the conversation later, but it should not be yours or my focus.

I know that we don't like to deal with being corrected about these things because we tend to think that we have some spirituality or insight, and we can say whatever we want to say to people. However, we don't have that right. We don't have all the answers, and we don't know all the reasons for all the whys. Perhaps you have experienced that people didn't know how to deal with your grief. You might have been in situations where people did the wrong things at the wrong time while you were grieving. You know people will approach you the wrong way when you're grieving. They make you feel you are wrong because you are grieving, and you should be stronger than that or you should be spiritual. I'm wondering if we understand that there's always a human side to our reaction to everything. Everything is not a spiritual reaction. We are human, so we react in human ways.

I got a call from a family member telling me my cousin's wife was dealing with cancer, and chemo and all treatments have stopped. We prayed for a miracle. I must admit to you, I felt some kind of way when I got that news that she wasn't recovering. It was the human side of me feeling that way, and there was nothing wrong with me feeling that way. It didn't mean I don't have faith or believe God. It didn't mean that I'm not praying. It just means that I'm human. I felt a certain kind of way when I got that news that nothing more could be done for her. I've been thinking about it and praying and telling God, we will go with whatever You do. If You heal, we thank You, but if you decide to do something different, we're going to thank You still. That's being human. **To be human means to feel and act with compassion.**

Jesus was often touched by the issues of our humanity, sickness, grief, and death. He was moved by compassion in the

Bible. Jesus was compassionate. That's where we have missed out when it comes to grieving and comforting hurt people. We don't show compassion. I know we want to have tough love. Tough love is appropriate at certain times, but not in all situations. We also need to have compassion. Learning to be compassionate when things happen helps us to know what not to do and what not to say. When you have compassion, you don't go into a room full of grieving family members talking crazy and asking them why you all in here crying and telling them to get over it. You need to have compassion.

Shortly after my mother-in-law passed, I posted on Facebook saying how we were going to miss her and what a great person she was. Suddenly, on my comment section, one of the preachers I grew up together with came on my timeline. He was talking crazy and ignorantly saying that I needed to take the post (mess) off because I am a man of God. Initially, I didn't mind him or that comment and went on, and didn't bother with it, but then he later in-boxed me and said crazier stuff. At that point, I blocked him from my page or contacts. I completely blocked him. I understood that even though he was a pastor, a man of God, he was dealing in ignorance. Since he's dealing in ignorance, my tolerance level for ignorance was extremely low in that place of grief. I don't deal with ignorance like that. I have the choice of whether I want to deal with it or not. My choice was to block him and not have anything to do with him.

What I am saying is, it was evident that this person

lacked compassion. The level of his ignorance and insensitivity were very high. My tolerance level for foolishness is very low. I've gotten older, and I don't put up with rude craziness. My mother-in-law had just passed. When I made the post, the coroner hadn't even come to pronounce her death, or take the body out of the home yet. Here's somebody making an ignorant statement. Please note, if you're a person that's supposed to know what you're doing in crisis or grief, whether you're a pastor or whomever, then know what to do and what to say with compassion. So, please stop doing that kind of foolishness. Let's ask God for wisdom on what to say to people and what not to say to people. Let's learn that and do better because we're living in such an insensitive day.

Here's some wisdom to help. Again, when people have lost their loved ones, if you don't know what to say, then don't say anything. If you don't know what to say, don't visit the house. If you don't know what to say, don't comment on Facebook. If you don't know what to say, just don't say anything. Don't do it. I mean, it's so elementary that my grandkids would know that. Just be quiet because the worst thing you can do when people are grieving is push the wrong button with your words. You are going to be got. They are going to get you. Something is coming out that you may not be ready for. I promise you that. You should learn not to do that.

When others are grieving, many people post pictures or videos on social media. They do a lot more expressing how they feel and trying to deal with their grief. Perhaps sometimes we don't understand why they are doing it, but if you don't understand, then don't comment. Your silence and prayers are better than the possibility of you saying the wrong thing at the wrong time. Be smart enough not to say the wrong stuff. If you're not smart enough to know otherwise, then be quiet. That's the smartest thing you can do.

When people are grieving the death of loved one, please let us not always try to connect death with the judgment of God. Everything is not judgment! Some things are natural occurrences. Death is something that happens every day. It doesn't mean that every time something happens to somebody, that it is God's judgment on their lives. That's also where we have been so insensitive. We presume everything is on God, that's God, that God did it, or that God is judging. I've seen people do that on social media. When COVID-19 first hit with this pandemic, some were saying God is cleaning the church. Then, when it hit their house, they changed that tune. I don't want to be insensitive, but I was saying, "Look, if God was cleaning the church with everyone else passing, now that COVID has hit your house and your loved ones died, God must still be cleaning the church". See how we can be insensitive until it hits us. You should have left that alone because you didn't understand what you were saying. You didn't know you were not the spokesperson for God on this matter anyway. You have been insensitive to other people. Now that it's hit you, you want all of us to feel sorry for you. Let's learn to be sensitive. Don't create a situation where you will have to experience this level of pain to be respectful of others and sensitive.

One of the worst things you can do when someone is grieving is to push them to make drastic changes when they are not ready yet. Grieving is a process. Even though people are functioning at some level doesn't mean they are ready to move on and make changes. For example, I know people whose parents have died years ago. However, they haven't even got rid of their clothes or things in the house. They're working their way to it and in time they will do it, but they haven't gotten to that place yet. So, are they bad people because they haven't gotten there to that place? No. So because we want them to hurry up, we feel it's our place to tell them to throw all their things out and move on? No! I encourage those who are grieving to keep those things as long as they need to. Eventually, they will sort it out.

When I first became the Pastor of Holy Trinity, which is now Restoration Revival Church of God in Christ, there was a picture right over the pulpit of the late Pastor Benton and his wife. Someone came to the church one day, and said to me, "Oh, no, you need to take that picture down. You are the Pastor now". They asked when I was going to take the picture down. I laughed and said, "No, I'm going to leave that picture right where it is". I left that picture right there. I had been the Pastor for two years when one day Mother Brown, one of the mothers who was there when I got there, came to me, and said, "Pastor, could I ask you a question?". I said, "Sure, mother". She asked, "When are you going to take that picture down?" She said, "You're the Pastor now. I think you should take it down now". I removed that picture then. If I had gone in and moved that picture while they were still grieving over the loss of their Pastor, it would have caused me problems, but wisdom said, "Do not move that picture until somebody that was already here says something about it". When they did, I moved the picture. They were grieving. The worst thing for me to do was go in, change everything and move that picture. I didn't even change the services right away. It took me a year before I started changing some things around. I didn't do anything suddenly. Why? Because they were still grieving the loss of a Pastor. When I finally started changing things, they were all in, with no resistance or disruption. **You don't handle grieving people certain ways that rush or push them into quick changes.** Let people decide when they are ready to release things and not you trying to direct them to move on now before they've come through the grieving process. Even though you may think it's therapy, and you may think it's good, you must pray and ask God how to handle the issue of change with those who are grieving. Everyone's different, so you don't handle everybody the same way.

We're not sensitive to people. We're not sensitive to God. We're not sensitive to the Spirit. We just say all kinds of crazy things that make no sense and injure people who are already hurting in grief. They've lost loved ones, sons and daughters, sisters and brothers, mothers, and fathers. Cut that out!! Learn to be sensitive to people. Learn how to deal with people. Go ahead and ask God to give you the tongue of the learned to know what to say and when to say it.

As mentioned before, love each other while we've got each other. Don't wait! I'm telling all of you right now, don't wait! If you love me, say so. Don't wait, tell me now. Call me now, text me now, email me now, inbox me now. Do all that now! Because when I'm gone, I can't hear a word you say. All the stuff you say may be excellent but tell it to me so I can hear it and say thank you.

Let others know what they mean to you now. Let's be more supportive of each other. Let's help to push each other. Let's help push each other's plans. I don't have to be the star. Let's help push each other to their goals, their destiny. Let's support. Sometimes I know we're tired, but let's support. I close with this. I will never forget the story that Patti LaBelle told when she was being interviewed. She was talking about one of her sisters that had passed. She had come home from off the road. She said she was so tired, but her sister wanted a chicken salad sandwich. She said, "Tell her I'll come and fix it for her tomorrow. I'll be by tomorrow to fix it". She said, when she woke up the following day, she got the message that her sister had passed. She said she had to live with that thing. She said she was tired, but she should have pressed to make that sandwich for her because she wanted it, not knowing she would not be there the next day. Let's stop putting off when someone asks us for something we really can do, especially if there's a reason they are asking at that time. If they ask to see you, don't put it off. Do it. You never know it could be the last time you see each other. Let's care for one another and love one another while we can. I pray that this will help us.

On a personal note, someone asked, "How do I handle a grieving spouse?" I think this wisdom can apply to any grieving family member, but this is my experience and observation that I think can help. I'm very careful to be mindful that my wife is grieving. My wife lost her mother in July 2020. She lost her sister on January, 2021. Just recently she lost another sister in March 2022. I must tell you that it's been a process. When she lost her mother, she was grieving. She and her mother talked every day. She called her mother every day, and this is no exaggeration. Her mother liked watching Joe Ligon and the Mighty Clouds of Joy videos. So, my wife gave her mother her iPad and set it up so she could watch stuff on YouTube. When they called and said that her mother wasn't responding like she was before in conversations and replies, I told my wife, "Your mother is transitioning". She immediately got some of her things together and said to me, "I won't be back until whenever" and she left the house and went over to mother's house. Lady Martin stayed there at her mother's house until her mother passed. When Mother Pace passed away, I went over, and we were there until they came and pronounced her dead, and then my wife came home.

When Duranice, her sister, was in the hospital, the last couple of days before her sister passed, Lady Martin talked to her every day. God gave us a nurse that worked there, and she was a Godsend. She helped my wife to be able to FaceTime and talk to her sister. We got a chance to talk to her before she transitioned. My wife told me the other day, "This one hurt even worse than my mother". She's had to deal with it. I don't know if there is a day that goes by that she doesn't watch her sister's video or listen to her music as she processes her grief. I've learned to deal with her carefully and not to be insensitive. You know, as men, sometimes we must admit, we will be like, "okay, let's move on," but no, you must learn to flow together as your spouse recovers, whether it's male or female. So be mindful, careful, and be sensitive. Sometimes they don't want to be bothered with seeing anyone. Sometimes they don't want to talk. Sometimes they're going to be in their own little world. You just have to know that. Sometimes my wife will feel the need to be with her sisters. I don't say you don't need to go. I encourage her to stay as long as she needs to, or as long as she wants to. That's the way I deal with her. If and when she's listening to her sister's music and I'm in the room, sometimes, I'll leave the room and just let her have that moment. One day, I walked into the room, and she was listening to something of her sister that somebody sent her, and she was crying. I just looked at her. She was repeating it over and over. I just politely backed out of the room and let her have that moment. Then, I later went back in to console her. We must understand that everyone deals with their grief differently. If it's your spouse that you have to deal with in their grief process, the best thing you can do is to learn them in their vulnerable place. Be sensitive in a way that you don't say the wrong thing or even the right things at the wrong time. One of the things I do intentionally is to try to keep her laughing. I try to do things that are funny, a positive distraction to give her mind a break from all the losses. I am just finding ways or creating ways to keep her uplifted. Why? Because I want to do that for her. My wife said to me one day, "I just need to get out of this house. I need to go someplace". I got her a hotel room, and she stayed for two days. That was therapy for her. This is what we must do sometimes. We must find ways to get out of the house, to get a change of view and environment. Sometimes, we all need that and sometimes we need to give our grieving spouse and others in grief their own space. Even if you need space. You need a moment from time to time in grief recovery. I'll put it to you this way. Give people space to be who they are and to deal with what they must deal with.

Here is an important key to dealing with grieving people when they need space. **Do not. I repeat, do not take it personal**. It has nothing to do with you or me. Don't be offended. Allow our spouses or others who are grieving to have their personal space to deal with where they are and what they feel. They will need uninterrupted space sometimes. In that place, they just may not want to be bothered. They may not want to talk at that moment. Don't try to hold a conversation when they don't feel like talking. Remember you know how you get when you don't feel like talking. You don't want to talk. I have days that I am okay. Then, I have days that I am not in a talkative mood. My family will say, "He doesn't feel like talking". Then, they leave me alone. Then, there are days they know, "Oh, he is talking and I'm just running my mouth". Give the griever their personal space. We must do that. I remind you, remember in this space, that you can't take everything personally. A reality check is that everything is not about you. Everyone's not talking about you. They are not thinking about you either. You are not the main focus. I mean it's not a personal thing. Know this and you'll avoid feeling hurt. I don't take anything personally. It may seem like it is, but it's not. You and your spouse or loved one will get through this and heal. I pray that this helps.

CHAPTER 11

THE CONVERSATION NOBODY WANTS TO HAVE

The conversation that no one likes to have is a conversation that doesn't involve people that have already passed. The discussion involves those of us that are still living. We want to avoid specific conversations about death and dying, but in the Bible, the Prophet came and told Hezekiah to get his house in order because he was soon going to die. He was told to get his affairs in order. The message was not only related to what he needed to do to prepare to die but also about Hezekiah's business affairs. Though most of us want to avoid such conversations, we need to have them with our loved ones, the people we trust. **Yes, have that conversation.** Some of you probably can recall when our older relatives, like my grandmother, met the insurance guy at our house every month. Every month, he had this little black case with papers in it. We didn't have ways to pay online back then, but my grandmother paid for a policy every month. During that time, the policy wasn't that much, but she paid it religiously. If she missed a payment, she figured out the means to pay and catch it up. She paid for those policies, and she ensured that we knew where those policies were in case anything happened to her. It was a conversation she had with us while we were teenagers. She told us that the policy is under her mattress. She showed us the policy and told us what we needed to do if anything ever happened. She told us that we would be taken care of and that they would be put away nicely. In these current times, we don't like to have that conversation, and we do not always have our business affairs in order, for when we die.

I remember back in 2011, a young lady called us, and she wanted to sell us a policy for burial. She came to the house, so I had her put Lady Martin and me into the policy. I later had her come back when my uncle was in town. I had her come and put him into a policy. Now I paid the policy every month for him out of my pocket, knowing that he was busy and on the road a lot. It wasn't always easy to pay, but I kept it paid. When I got the call that he had passed, the first call or the second call I made after that was to the insurance company, and they got the information they needed. We put the process in place to go to the funeral home, and set up his service, and purchase his casket. We did all that, and it was a smooth process. We did not have to raise any money because his funeral costs had been taken care of. Not only had we put those matters in place, but my cousin Michelle and my uncle had already picked out a plot. They picked out a family plot, where most of my aunts and relatives and my mother are buried. They bought those plots early. When he passed, arrangements were smooth because they were planned out and prepared for before his death.

Think about this. If you had to go into the hospital, and something were to happen to you, do people know where to find your important information? Will they know? If you are too ill to respond and make decisions for yourself, how can you give someone the Power of Attorney? Who will speak for you? Do you have a medical living will on file? When my mother-in-law got sick, and the doctor had sent her home, he gave her a couple of weeks to live. She called a meeting one day, and they had a young lady come over, and they started talking about her burial plots, as she wanted to be buried next to her husband and son. They signed the paperwork and gave someone the power of attorney to handle matters just in case something happened to her. When she closed her eyes, everything was already settled and planned out, even down to her homegoing ceremony by her own design. When she passed away, the family was able to go through the process smoothly to bury her and get those things done that she wanted and needed them to do.

Another important conversation is about provisions and who has access to the information. Both those aspects are important. My wife and I have life insurance, and we both have access to those important papers. Also, the business administrator at church where I am pastor knows this information too. Thanks be to God, and I praise His holy name, that I didn't pass in August from COVID-19, but if I had, they would have had no strain trying to find all the information they needed to settle things. I have a list of all my online accounts and put them in a safe place so that if something happened to me, they could get to them without going through changes. If I became sick, was in a coma, or otherwise was too sick to respond, the matters of paying the mortgage, other bills, and addressing my responsibilities could continue without a problem for anyone. Our parents and older relatives taught us the value of those particular conversations and thinking ahead and putting things in place. I want to encourage you to make this a priority too. If you sometimes spend a lot of money on other items, I encourage you to make it a priority to find you an insurance company that has good coverage. Be diligent, and research the different types of insurance to find what will be best for you and your family. I've got insurance on all my grandkids, and I pay it every month. It's automatically drafted out of my account. God forbid that anything happens, but you've got to be prepared in case anything happens. Get life insurance enough to cover your final arrangements and then some. You don't want to leave your family in a situation where they have to start a GoFundMe account. Lady Martin is the beneficiary of my policy. She gets the money. Someone foolish once said they were not leaving any money behind for their wife to spend on another man. You are not going to be here to know how your spouse will spend the money anyway. The wedding vows say, "Until death do us part." Well at death, we part. If I leave Lady Martin a $500,000 policy, and she spends it upon my death on another guy, who cares? I mean, I'll be enjoying heaven. Who she spends it on doesn't even matter. Don't be selfish or crazy. When your family is in jeopardy because you have passed away and did not handle your business, you put them in harm's way and create hardship for them. Put a living will in place too, whether you're young or old. Being young does not guarantee we're going to be here forever.

We need to think that way. We don't want to leave our families and our loved ones with financial hardship, trying to bury us and struggling to get funds. It takes preparation to get these things together before we do buy or invest in some other things in life. We need to look at this seriously and start this conversation.

I know someone who wrote out their full service. They wrote it out and listed who they wanted on the program. Mother Pace put her program together and called us to the house to go over all of it while her grave plot was finalized. When some asked why I was preaching Mother Pace's service, I informed them that it was because she had told me to. She made an announcement to tell everyone that Pastor Martin was to preach her eulogy if something were to happen to her. That announcement took place about a year and a half before she passed, but she knew what she wanted. You can reduce confusion by certain actions that you take. For example, having a <u>Will</u> made can avoid a lot of fights, confusion, and disagreements.

Sometimes people will try to tell you that they are getting ready to leave here, and we don't want to hear. They already know because they've sensed that it's their time. We brush them off like nothing is going to happen, but sometimes, it does happen. Don't hesitate, and don't be afraid to have important conversations. Death is a natural thing. Unless the Lord delays His coming, or the rapture takes place, all of us are going to leave this earth by death one day. Think about the fact that we've had almost a million people die from COVID-19 in the USA, and people are still getting sick and dying with other issues too. I am urging you to put your affairs in place. Get insurance. You may not use it, but at least you have it in place. It's like your car insurance. Once you have it, you may never have a wreck, but you pay for it every month so when or if you need it, you are covered. Get some health insurance. It's out there, so we have no excuse. When I was admitted to the hospital for COVID-19 last August, I was and am grateful that I had insurance. If I hadn't had that insurance, who knows what could have happened? They sent me a summary of a bill for ten days of being in the hospital. That bill was $97,000! Do you hear what I said? It was $97,000! That's not including all the other specialized costs. I was so grateful to have good insurance that allowed me to get the best treatment and follow-ups with the best doctors. Thank God for Obamacare, as they call it. It was a good thing.

Get your house in order. This includes your spiritual house, and your domestic affairs too. Everyone needs to understand that these things are necessary. Too much is happening, and too many are leaving, for us to avoid having these conversations. Make sure that people know what's going Have the conversation, make plans, do what you must do. It's important. It will bless you. May God bless you and may all God's choice blessings be yours.

ABOUT THE AUTHOR

God has always sought for a man to stand in the gap and build a hedge to turn away His wrath from men; a man who is willing to sell out for Him, lay everything and himself on the altar. One who will follow Him in righteousness and live holy; one who is willing to present himself as a living sacrifice for the Lord's work. God found a young man in Atlanta, Georgia, who was willing to be a yes man: Yes, I will preach; Yes, I will plant the seed of truth in the hearts of men that will make them free.

Contrary to popular belief, all of our young men are not in prison or on drugs. Some of them are endeavoring to make a difference in the world. Certainly, this is the case with Pastor Martin. He was saved at a early age, and filled with the Holy Ghost. At the age of 16, he received his commission from God to "Go ye into all the world and preach the gospel." He has traveled extensively around the country ministering the "Good News" of our Lord and Saviour Jesus Christ full time since 1979 with the Action Revival Team, under the auspices of Evangelist Gene Martin, and as a national Evangelist with the Church of God in Christ since 1986. Many souls have been saved and delivered through his ministry as he has prayed the prayer of faith. The Lord has touched the hearts of the old and young through his ministry.

Pastor Martin is CEO of Restoration Revival Ministries, and the pastor of Restoration Revival Church of God in Christ in East Point, Georgia. He served as State President of the Department of Evangelism for the Central Georgia Jurisdiction from 1992 until 1999. In December 2000, the late Presiding Bishop G. E. Patterson and General Board appointed him First Vice President of the International Department of Evangelism, and January 2005, he was appointed President of the Department where he served until January 2009. Pastor Martin was appointed Administrative Assistant to Bishop Norman O. Harper, South Central Georgia Jurisdiction in December 2011. He is uniquely articulate and highly respected among his peers. His ministry represents the spirit of excellence.

Aside from his other functions, he is a sustainer and loving husband to his wife of forty-three years, Evangelist June-Pace Martin, one of the "Anointed" Pace Sisters, and a role model to his daughter, Anthalena Patrice Martin and son, Dennis L. Martin, II and daughter in love Mae Martin and granddaughter Madison Martin, grandson Dennis (D3) Martin, III and granddaughter Rylee Martin and grandson King Lamar Martin.